TRANQUEBAR PRESS
IN THE HOT UNCONSCIOUS

Charles Foster is a Fellow of Green Templeton College,
University of Oxford.

He has written, edited or contributed to over thirty-five
books on many subjects, including travel, evolutionary
biology, natural history, anthropology, theology,
archaeology, philosophy and law. He says, 'They are all
attempts to answer the questions, "who or what are we?"
and "what on earth are we doing here?"' Recent publications
include *Wired for God? The Biology of Spiritual Experience*; *The
Sacred Journey*; *The Misadventures of Mr Badshot*; *The Selfless
Gene; Choosing Life, Choosing Death*; and *Human Dignity in
Bioethics and Law*.

Foster is married with six children, and lives in Oxford. His
website is www.charlesfoster.co.uk

## PRAISE FOR *IN THE HOT UNCONSCIOUS*

'Foster must by now be the greatest living travel writer in the English-speaking world. His vision is both extraordinarily acute and astonishingly wide, his prose tumbling forth like a lava flow straight from some muse of fire, hitting the page so hot that you can smell the scorching rocks and find yourself ducking for cover. Yet, not content with writing about India more evocatively, fondly, quizzically, searchingly, vibrantly, and, at times, comically than anyone I have ever read, he has also written here one of the finest tales of self-exploration, a work of deep spiritual questioning that is as unstuffy and full of life as the teeming Hindu temples he encounters, with their erotic carvings, gibbering monkeys and ancient holy men. You are constantly taken by surprise by this exuberant, but ruthlessly self-aware, account of the most unconventional and riveting of pilgrimages. Indeed, can one call it a pilgrimage at all, this wild journey that starts, characteristically enough, with a quest for giant leeches, and ends leaving the great questions, as it must, (almost) unanswered?'

– **Iain McGilchrist, author of** *The Master and His Emissary:*
*The Divided Brain*

~

'Charles Foster has accomplished a rare thing. He has managed to write a book about religion that is funny, witty, totally irreverent, completely pleasurable, and utterly profound. Chesterton said, "It is a test of a good religion whether you can make a joke about it." He must have had someone like Foster in mind. Highly recommended. I couldn't put it down.'

– **Larry Dossey, M.D., author of** *Healing Words:*
*Reinventing Medicine*

~

'This fascinating, quirky, finely written book will take you deep into the sometimes fierce challenges that are encountered in an authentic East-West dialogue. Charles Foster is an original and passionate guide to the rewards and difficulties that arise through confronting the reality of India and its great tradition.'

— **Andrew Harvey, author of** *A Journey in Ladakh*

~

'*In the Hot Unconscious* is both a fascinating spiritual memoir and a picaresque travelogue. Though steeped in the traditions of East and West, and willing to go to great, even painful lengths in search of wisdom, Foster is much funnier and much more aware of the traps of ego than most writer-seekers who have found themselves in India. The result is as poetic and moving as it is humorous.'

— **Jonathan Foreman, Executive Editor,** *Indian Quarterly*

~

# In The Hot Unconscious
## AN INDIAN JOURNEY

Charles Foster

TRANQUEBAR

TRANQUEBAR PRESS
An imprint of westland ltd
Venkat Towers, 165, P.H. Road, Maduravoyal, Chennai 600 095
No. 38/10 (New No.5), Raghava Nagar, New Timber Yard Layout, Bangalore 560 026
Survey No. A-9, II Floor, Moula Ali Industrial Area, Moula Ali, Hyderabad 500 040
23/181, Anand Nagar, Nehru Road, Santacruz East, Mumbai 400 055
4322/3, Ansari Road, Daryaganj, New Delhi 110 002

First published in TRANQUEBAR by westland ltd 2012

10 9 8 7 6 5 4 3 2 1

ISBN: 978-93-81626-50-4

Typeset by *Kumar Raman*, New Delhi

Printed at Gopsons Paper Ltd., Noida

For sale in the Indian sub-continent only

*For Mary,*
*my best friend and fellow traveller*
*&*
*for Pramod,*
*the singing boy on the rock*

'We take a handful of sand from the endless landscape of awareness around us, and call that handful of sand the world.'

— Robert M. Pirsig

*Zen and the Art of Motorcycle Maintenance*

~

'Reason's last step is the recognition that there is an infinite number of things that are beyond it. It is merely feeble if it does not go as far as to realise that. If natural things are beyond it, what are we to say about supernatural things?'

— Blaise Pascal

*Pensees, no. 267*

~

'There are differences, sometimes very radical differences, between East and West....But I know now that there is a dialogue possible between the truths of East and West, a dialogue of extraordinary beauty and complexity. Perhaps, from that dialogue, which we are only just beginning, will come truths as yet unformed and unglimpsed by either East or West, truths that may, in some way none of us can foresee, fuse the dynamic intuitions and practice of Western philosophy and science and the transcendental insight of the East. Sometimes, when I am in despair, I think that to pursue this dialogue seriously is the last hope for the West to listen not merely to Eastern voices, but to its own buried and banished voices, the voices it has silenced at its peril — the voices of Plato, of Dante, of Eckhart — all those voices that speak of ecstasy and the long labour of the spirit.'

— Andrew Harvey

*A Journey in Ladakh*

~

'Ancient man, that is man from the earliest times until the first millennium before Christ (and even after that in the greater part of the world until the present day) lived in the world of the imagination, that is the world of integral wholeness. Of this world of the imagination the supreme expression was the Myth. Myth is a symbolic utterance which arises from the depths of the unconscious, or rather from the deep levels of consciousness which lie below the level of rational consciousness. The rational mind, with its abstract concepts and logical constructions, is like the tip of an iceberg, while below it are vast levels of consciousness which link our human nature with the universe around us, and with the archetypes or transcendent principles which govern the Universe. The Myth is the reflection in the human imagination of these archetypal ideas, those cosmic principles and powers, which were known in the ancient world as the gods or angels.'

— Bede Griffiths
*The Marriage of East and West*

∽

'...Jesus called for them and said: 'Let the little children come to me, and do not stop them; for it is to such as these that the kingdom of God belongs. Truly I tell you, whoever does not receive the kingdom of God as a little child will never enter it....'

— Luke 18:16

∽

# CONTENTS

# ACKNOWLEDGEMENTS

My debts are many and immense.

The greatest debt is to the people I met on these travels, who, with a few dishonourable exceptions, were patient, courteous, dignified and fun. For reasons that will be obvious, I have often changed the names of people and places. Dr Shankar, in particular, is an unrecognisable amalgam of people. He's not to be found anywhere.

The northern India trip was substantially funded by St John's College, Cambridge, who were no doubt deeply disappointed at how little serious research there was. Sorry.

David Monteath read the entire manuscript in draft and made a number of penetrating observations.

My editor at Tranquebar, Dharini Bhaskar, has been amazing: patient, efficient and perceptive. The book is much, much better for her work.

My agent, Anuj Bahri, faced with an eccentric project, saw what I was trying to get at. Many agents would have missed the point entirely. I'm very grateful for his faith and confidence.

The book was written in huts, cafés and railway carriages in India, in Anne and Iain's Norrie's flat in Edinburgh, and in the Codrington Library of All Souls College, Oxford. I had unfailing hospitality and help in all these places, apart from one of the railway carriages.

My family always bears the brunt of long foreign trips. I'm not really sure why I keep travelling, but I'm immensely grateful (I think), that my wife Mary puts up with it so cheerfully, and unequivocally glad that my children have so far always run gleefully to me when I get back.

Where an unattributed quote appears at the start of a chapter, it is a *koan* commonly used in the Buddhist (and particularly the Zen) community. Usually they are ancient; often their origins are obscure.

The extracts from *The Four o'Clock Talks,* Father Bede's introduction to *Psalms for Christian Prayer*, and Father Bede's *Falling in Love with India* are reproduced with the kind permission of Brother Martin and Saccidananda Ashram, Shantivanam.

# PREFACE

This is a tale of my own confusion. The plot is simple enough. I went to India, was confused, and then came back. It is also an attempt to see whether or not confusion matters.

Most of the stories here are concerned at one level or another with how myths are made, and therefore how myths can be evaluated.

The book is written with a number of rather obvious preconceptions, two unshakeable convictions, and several shakeable and regularly shaken beliefs. The first unshakeable conviction is that the act of living as a human being is itself a religious act. There's nothing we can do to make it less religious, although there's a lot that we can and do do to make it less religiously satisfactory. The second unshakeable conviction is that, as human beings, we're all missing out massively on things that we desperately need.

'I hope it's not going to be a religious book,' said my father. Well, it is, I'm afraid. If human living is necessarily religious, I suppose there's no such thing as a non-religious book. Some parts of this book are even *about* religion. I challenge anyone to write a book about India that isn't.

I juxtapose Christianity (as opposed to any other creed) with Eastern religion partly because of my personal history, and partly because modern Christianity's (unhistoric) insistence on belief rather than praxis makes it the best example of religious left-brained-ness. No other religion has creeds like Christianity. Relatively few Jews, for instance, believe in Maimonides' supposedly foundational 'Thirteen Principles of Faith', and no one thinks that a Jew is not Jewish if he can't subscribe to them all. Some other religions do demand affirmations of belief, but in no case are they anything like as metaphysically complex as Christianity's; in no case is what one does and what one is, so subservient to what one believes. It is for that reason, amongst many others, that I am happier in Jerusalem than Rome, let alone than in Tennessee. But that's another story.

There is a bitter competition between Christianity and the religions of the East. Amongst educated Westerners the play is all one way: Christianity is all but defeated. Cocktails of Hinduism and Buddhism, mixed with amorphous New Age mysticism from other sources, are the spiritual drink of choice in Hampstead and New York.

There are many reasons why this has happened. One important reason is that Christianity – and particularly Western Protestant Christianity – has signally failed to satisfy the right-brain's thirst for mystery, intuitive spirituality and the numinous. Indeed Protestant Christianity has often said that it is dangerously illegitimate to have a craving for such things. It is often and rightly said that the oppressive masculine has crushed the sacred feminine. But asserting this dichotomy itself has its dangers. Men who aren't in this sense feminine too aren't proper men.

The view that mysticism is illegitimate is a relatively recent one in the history of the church. There is (of course) a vibrant tradition of mysticism in the Church, which is still influential in the Roman and Orthodox churches. An unlettered Coptic monk would be able to talk much more meaningfully to a Hindu sadhu than a modern conservative Protestant with a degree in mission studies. The view is deadly, deadly dull, and dead wrong. We are built for ecstasy, and waste away if we don't get it. The prognosis for Western Protestantism will remain dire as long as it is run by men (and it is mostly *men*) who switch off a Mozart symphony, asking loudly: 'What's it *for?*', or who think that poetry, surfing, lovemaking, bird watching or just messing about with friends are unfortunate (if not actually demonic) distractions from the real business of Bible study or proselytism.

Bede Griffiths talked about the need for a marriage of East and West, and if he meant marriage in the 'one body' sense, then he was spot on. Anything less than that won't do. A happy coalition or respectful discussion falls dangerously short. I'm not advocating some sort of intellectually uncomfortable syncretism. It's not honest and it's not remotely radical enough. Full consummation is urgently needed if we're to have any chance of wholeness. But there's no need for the West to get a plane to Chennai for the consummation. After all, Christianity is an Eastern religion that just happens to speak Greek.

**– Charles Foster, Oxford**

*February 2012*

~

## Chapter 1

# THE RIGHT ARM OF ST THOMAS

*'The truth knocks on the door and you say, "Go away, I'm
looking for the truth," and so it goes away.'*
— Robert M. Pirsig
*Zen and the Art of Motorcycle Maintenance*

∽

I met Basmati Jenkins down by the Chinese fishing nets in
Fort Cochin. He was eating ice cream, reading a glossy
religious magazine with a very anatomical diagram of the
Sacred Heart of Jesus on the cover, and he only had one eye,
which looked mildly out through thick pink glasses.

We got talking when he dropped his ice cream on his
lap. I offered him the business pages of *The Hindu* to wipe it
up with. His thanks were fulsome, and peppered with
invocations of some very exotic Portuguese saints. When he
heard I was from England, he asked me how devoted the UK
government was to the memory of the Tyburn Martyrs. 'Not

much, to be honest,' I replied. He shook his head in disappointment, and his glasses fell off. I picked them out of the gutter, wiped them down with a feature on wife-beating, and handed them back. The thanks began again. 'You must come to my house.' And so, being a fool, I went.

He led me off down Bazaar Street, past the tea and spice and rice merchants, past the Mattancherry Palace, and into a little alley in Jew Town, filled with stale air and resentful cats. 'Just wait a moment, please,' he said, and urinated into an open drain. He pointed along his stream. 'See that,' he said. 'There, at the end of my arc. The rat. That was only the size of a guinea pig when it died on Tuesday. Now it looks like a beaver. It's an amazing climate, this.' I looked nervously for the exits, but his mother was leaning over the balcony and beckoning us up.

The house was a shrine. Every inch of the peeling wall was covered in religious lithographs. In the kitchen, incense spiralled up before a plaster statue of a detached St Anthony, calmly looking at the arrows that bloodlessly pierced him. Presiding over the dining table was a huge, fleshy, vacant Madonna holding a child of astonishing ugliness. Gregorian chants from a monastery in Burgundy crackled out of a cassette player. Pope John Paul II raised his hands to bless anyone going down the fire escape to the toilet in the hot yard outside.

We sat in silence as the vegetable curry and chapattis were carried in. Basmati's father followed them, bowed to the Virgin and then to me, crossed himself, said a long grace in Latin, and started to eat in silence.

'Father,' said Basmati. 'This is my friend. He comes from Oxford – the city of John Henry Newman.'

'Newman was a good man,' said the father, and continued to eat. The silence was broken only by the screaming of a cat dying loudly under the wheels of a rickshaw. At the end of the meal the father belched, crossed himself again, stood up and said to Basmati, 'You must take him to Kodangallur.'

We went the next day, driving north along Kerala's main coast road, over bridges spanning the languid backwaters, through exhaustingly fecund banana and coconut palm plantations. Always, even in the suffocating gridlock of Ernakulum, the sea seethes away near the front of your consciousness; sucking and killing and crushing and sustaining.

It was across this sea that St Thomas the Apostle – the once-Doubting Thomas – is said to have come, landing in 52 AD at the then-bustling port of Muziris. Most of Muziris sank into the sand and was overwhelmed by the jungle, but there has always been a remnant, hanging on to the green killing coast and to the memories of old glories. The ghosts of the Greek and Roman and Arab traders who made Muziris great are hard to hear in the dowdy little town of Kodangallur, which stands on the ruins of Muziris. Their voices are drowned by the clinking of the chai stalls and the stutter of the scooters and the wind that moves the palms like grass.

It's possible that Thomas came here. The tradition that he did is a genuinely ancient one, but the antiquity of the tradition is the only real evidence. Certainly there was a good deal of trade between the Middle East and Muziris in the middle of the first century, spurred by the discovery in the 40s AD of a spectacular wind that swept ships fast from the Arabian peninsula to India. Thomas was the disciple who would not believe without satisfying himself of the evidence, but evidence has nothing at all to do with the unshakeable local belief in the historicity of his visit.

'This is the most important place in the whole of Mother India,' said Basmati, as our car wound round the little red lanes south of Kodangallur. 'This is where the redemption of India began.'

We turned into a drive that led by a wharf on a deep inlet. Opposite the wharf was an immense church, decorated with scenes from the life of St Thomas. Bus-loads of well-scrubbed Catholic school children walked obediently in lines, patrolled by sweating nuns in black serge habits. A boat was disgorging a cargo of pilgrims. A bookshop peddled absolute certainties in many languages. Crows pecked at pizza. A caretaker, slumped in a plastic chair, slapped his face and killed a fly. He wiped its body on his trousers.

'Come,' said a reverently excited Basmati, taking my arm and pulling me towards the church. It was almost empty. A monk looked at us suspiciously and unwrapped some chewing gum, as if to wash the taste of us away.

'Here,' said Basmati, 'here it is.' He gestured towards a reliquary, and fell on his knees.

Inside that box, if the custodians of the tradition are right, is the right arm of St Thomas. If they are right, there's a 50 per cent chance that this was the arm that reached out towards the wounds of the Risen Jesus.

On the face of it, Thomas was an ironic choice for India. Why send the arch-rationalist to the place which, more than any other, lives in the Unconscious? 'Always one comes back to this,' wrote Bede Griffiths, the Benedictine monk who set up a Christian ashram in Tamil Nadu and strove to broker a marriage between East and West: 'India still lives from the unconscious. In a sophisticated film they may relegate it to the madhouse, but it cannot be escaped. It is the heart of India. I feel this deep communion in the unconscious wherever I go. I just cease to live on the conscious level and let my whole being sink into the unconscious, the life of the sun pouring down from the sky and the life surging in these brown bodies, in their eyes and faces and movements and gestures. Speech seems unnecessary; it takes place on the surface. Beneath the surface is the vibrant life of the sun, of the blood, of a deep intelligence (everywhere I get the impression of a living intelligence; I have never seen such intelligent faces). I believe that there is also a deep awareness of God, not in the sense of a conscious being, but of the Infinite, the eternal, the One beyond consciousness....'

The passionate Peter would have been a more obvious choice for the India job. Or even the turbulent but sublime religious poet, Paul, who had showed at the Areopagus his ability to sympathise with and deploy strategically the devotional literature of other religions. Was this a case of God deliberately choosing the most unsuitable candidate in order to make some point about the Kingdom being a topsy-turvy, paradoxical place? Or was it a cunning divine strategy to smuggle reason into the temple of the unconscious; to brew in the immense cauldron of India the perfect synthesis of the rational and the intuitive; to wrench back into proper relationship the dislocated principles of Western, linear, masculine thought and Eastern, cyclical, feminine wisdom, so that humans could move again in the way they were designed to do?

Whether this was the plan or not, the reconciliation is vital and urgent, for Christianity and for every individual. When I first went to India, many years before, I didn't know (although I had begun to feel) the importance and the urgency. I was even more arrogant and ignorant than I am now, which is saying a lot. It was long before any of the reconciliation had begun in me. I went then to the north.

~

## Chapter 2

# APPROACHES

'Question 4. Master and pupil waited for a bus. A bus arrived: it was full and went on. "There'll be another soon," said the pupil. Said the master, "There will be no more." "But I know there will," said the pupil. "Fool!" said the master, hitting him over the head with his brolly. "Oh," said the pupil, "I see what you mean. The road is wide indeed." "That's better," said the master, as another bus arrived. Which bus did they get into?'

– Zen question in Christmas Humphreys
*A Western Approach to Zen*

∽

The flatlands of northern India are not tired like European floodplains There's a vertiginous feeling that something big or terrible is about to happen. Perhaps it's not surprising. The water oozing out of the hill is holier than the water of the great Ganges itself: it has just burst out of the mouth of Shiva, who squats in the high Himal. It sheds sanctity in its long crawl to the sea. The murky trickles in the paddies of the bleak north give a better brand of redemption than the sacred water at the Varanasi ghats.

Cranes screamed in the fields. An egret stabbed a snake. The bus stopped in a market in one of the old British hill-stations. A bean seller leaned against a red post-box, paring his nails with a steak knife. An office snored. The peaks to the south were pimples, the museum had shut in 1959, and the brothel was said to be the most deadly in Uttar Pradesh. Monkeys chattered over a concrete temple. To the north a green rampart reared up towards Tibet. My road burrowed into it.

The whitewashed wall next to my bed was pocked with bloodstains where other travellers had burst bed bugs. As I closed the window against the moths, a crowd of naked children scattered giggling into the trees, leaving nose prints on the glass in the silver dust of moth wings. The night was frantic.

I sat in the square, and a vision of Californian loveliness, soon to be named as Carly, simmered over towards me. I bought her some tea. India's a really spiritual place, I thought, so after she'd told me about her father's failing auto-insurance business, the first of her abortions and her distrust of the Catholic nuns who'd beaten the Nicene Creed into her with the back of a hairbrush, I thought I'd set out my stall. I knew her sort.

'I'd like you to know,' I said, leaning over the table, 'that I share your suspicion of dualism. But my problem is more with its popular pastiche than with the idea itself. Isn't a sort of dualism – flowing ultimately from a Judaeo-Christian understanding of the Creator-creature relationship – essential for asserting, preserving and enhancing the magnificent individual that is Carly? You are distinct from God, and – mercifully for you – distinct from Charles Foster. That's me, by the way, and it's splendid to meet you.'

She smiled. 'I have a suspicion of dualism?'

'Well of course you do. Isn't that why we're all here?'

'Okay. Right.'

'So you have, in a way denied by the oneness-of-us-all notions of the East, a unique status and space in which to be *you*. Your flourishing and your ultimate salvation consist in being more and more Carly, not less. Spiritual progress isn't a dissolution of Carly: not a blending of Carly with the rest of the universe: but rather her apotheosis. Of course as you become more and more you, you'll feel a growing solidarity with the rest of the creation. And no doubt some of the language of non-duality language will tend to spring to your lips to describe that solidarity. But the solidarity will be coming from a real relationship with the creation. And to relate you need to be *you*. The more *you* you are, the better a relater you'll be. It is the otherness of the beloved that is the real staple of true love.'

'You're trying to get into my knickers,' she said. Which wasn't the whole story.

By noon the next day, I was in a misty tangle of pines and rhododendrons before the blinding blue-white of the high snows.

I never wanted to come to India. It never had the resonance for me that central Africa has, or South America might be able to conjure. As a child in Yorkshire, I lay awake, shivering at the lions crawling round my bed, and woke to shoot kudu at the waterhole where they drank each morning, heads down beside the rocking horse. The milkman was the advance guard of the Zulu army covered with a popgun from behind the study curtains. And Alison, from the house across the valley, was the great pale queen holding the jewels of Sheba.

I knew that India was painted in bright colours. Knew it, but never saw the colours. I knew that there were fine things done there in red coats, and that the bazaars of the plains and the passes of the hills were the playgrounds of the Great Game. I knew that somewhere the sea, blown by a spiced wind, broke in hot foam on a beach made of shark bones. I knew that in a cave plastered with ice, a thin man with a skewer through his cheeks sat smiling, and that on a holy mountain birds the colour of cobalt were as thick on the flowers as flies on the face of a corpse. I knew this, but there was none of the piercing longing that there was for the thorn bush of Africa; no abiding wistfulness for the place. I was embarrassed by this. I felt I should do better – should feel more. I learned the map and recited the 'Ballad of East and West'. Then I gave up. And eventually I went to Africa, and was captured by it, and thought little more of India. So, then, I never really wanted to come to India.

I should have stayed away. There was no point in going

there without understanding something of the metaphysical mechanics of myth. I would have learned that better with my own native myths of hay-cropping, Green Men and river gods. I should have been taught by a laughing girl with cider-breath and fumbling hands, under a summer oak. Instead, for that vital part of my education, I was ushered alone (accompanied only by my many and corrosive prejudices), into the company of the alien, inaccessibly strange gods of Hinduism, and so it took me years longer to learn the basic grammar of the subject.

～

The Indian national flag strained straight in a hot wind – a wind that didn't ebb or flow or dance but pressed solidly against the teetering north wall of India. A child, carrying a brass pan of dal, went with the wind to a far corner of the square and ladled the mess out to the grandfather, who crouched under a blanket. The old man didn't look up. His tin plate was already in his hands. He must have heard the boy arrive, and felt the weight of the dal. But the child was irrelevant to him. The wind might have brought the food.

By the low wall, a gobbing paan seller shuffled in a spiral of damp dust, clutching his army greatcoat at the throat. He laughed when he saw me sitting at the café table, writing with one hand and tilting a tea cup in the other. 'They are very secure, these Indians,' I wrote.

A dead goat bubbled, fermented and rolled in the well.

A plated troop of beetles marched to one side of the well-head. My footfall quivered through them. The leader froze and wavered, waving metallic claws. I was still for a while, and there was confidence again.

Two stone gods copulated mournfully near the Mogul battlements; another watched them with baleful agate eyes. 'Give us sewers,' said the graffiti on the peeper's buttocks. And then, copied from one of the careful tapestries done by desperate Raj ladies pretending that they were in Eastbourne, 'Cleanliness is next to godliness.'

'Which god is cleanliness next to?' I fatuously asked my friend. He smiled wearily. A whitewashed wall proclaimed primly that 'Sangeet's reproductive organs are large and red', and that 'Kuldip's dhoti is soiled'.

As V.S. Naipaul noted, Indian defaecation is iconic. The Mahatma himself bemoaned the loss of all the fertilising potential of a billion Indian bowels: potential dissipated everywhere but into the soil of the villages. Dissipated into gutters, onto balconies, in hotel lobbies, on beaches, into birdbaths. Naipaul wonders at the yogic contortions which make it possible to defaecate into a urinal. I wonder at the cultic devotion to the activity. India is the land of the unembarrassed hitch of the dhoti. And pin-striped bottoms join the chatty fellowship of street-side evacuations. Caste is forgotten. The rectum is a great leveller. And there will always, eventually, be a sweeper to scratch up the results with a handful of willow twigs, or the thin dogs which, in the poorer villages, gather behind a crouching child. Some

Hindus sermonise and mythologise the business of dung. Here, in a drain, is the whole fecund circle of karma. In dead vegetables, squeezed through a colon, is the fertilising power that can cause differently incarnated things to spring towards the sun before dying themselves and entering the circle.

Jimi Hendrix beamed out from the sweeper's head scarf. She swung a foot or so to each side of her with the broom, cutting a slim path of lightly disturbed dust around the base of the wall. She came to an empty drink can. She knocked it to the side of her trail and went on. She did the same, further on, with a light bulb, a used syringe and a mouse. Nobody minded. Her patch was the strip by the wall. The square itself was her brother's territory. Everyone knew where they stood. Everyone knew the boundaries of responsibility. If her brother had done her job for her she would have been as unhappy and insecure as if she had been asked to do his.

It's wrong to say that caste suppresses personality. It guarantees it. In hard pressed societies, personality is defined in terms of function. You are what you do, or what you don't do. Caste is one thing. But there are equally bold distinctions within the castes. These distinctions preserve a unique niche for every human being. The woman swept this six inch strip. She was, unchallengeably and unchangeably, the sweeper of that strip. The sweeper of that strip is what she was. No one else on earth or, importantly, in heaven, could do that job, could *be* that. That was a comforting guarantee of temporal and eternal identity.

I said this to my friend, who was a learned Hindu. It was a strain for him to pity me as much as he had to.

'You've got hold of completely the wrong end of a very big stick.'

He settled back into the *London Review of Books*. No more discussion was needed. I waited. He looked up, saw me watching him, and looked down again, waggling himself deeper into the chair and concentrating improbably on the history of legal wig-making.

'Why?'

He looked up again. I must have looked earnest. He sighed, and folded up the *LRB*. He now looked dutiful.

'O son of Kunti, you who have asked me such difficult questions, know that it is just the light caressing of the instruments of sense which make the music that we call cold and heat, pain and pleasure. It is these that come and go. They do not endure. You must bear with them, O son of Bharata.'

This was obviously not addressed directly to me. My father is called Bryan, for a start, and this was wooden quoting.

'Who said that?'

'The Lord Krishna.'

'Go on.'

'But do you not understand?'

'Not exactly.'

He drew a deep breath and began again. 'You must know that the great That, which penetrates into and between everything which there is, is indestructible; no one and nothing can destroy that changeless Being.'

He stopped and looked hopefully at me. I shook my head. Resigned now, he continued:

'It is only the bodies of the Body-Dwellers, themselves undying, infinite and everlasting, which have an end. It is for this reason that you fight, O son of Bharata.' There was a pause. 'Yes?' he said.

'No.'

'It is very simple. It is elementary stuff. But you can be forgiven for your ignorance.'

'You are very kind.'

'It is a mighty paradox. That the simplest is the most complex. That the jewel is in the heart of the lotus, which is sweet, and in every puddle.'

I frowned, and shrugged, and he was offended. He went defensively on. 'We are not what we *do* at all. But instead we only *are* when we do nothing at all. The acts that you think so important, the little crazy busy-nesses, are far from being the essence of the actor. They cloud the vision of the Absolute. They prevent the person *being*. To the extent that a person *does*, he is not.' He had stopped speaking in his Indian way. There were no underlinings, qualifications, superlatives or dizzying circumlocutions. He spoke in clipped Socratic sentences.

At its best, Indian speech incarnates the cyclic presumptions of Indian philosophy, and those presumptions mirror the slow-turning buffalo cartwheel of existence on which the Indian personality is nailed, joyfully or agonisingly. But there were no incarnate presumptions in this cold

Athenian talk. With the presumptions had gone the warm, globular feel of Indian conversation, the woolliness that makes you feel that all can find a bed here. I was disappointed, because I'm an eternal tourist, and I like the picturesque. He saw this, knew he was being patronised, but ploughed graciously on.

'To comprehend is to be mistaken. To be a victim of the very *maya*, the very illusion, that you think you are comprehending. You can only properly grasp reality by *apprehending* it. One stumbles across the Absolute when one least expects it is there. One bumps into reality. One does not discuss it.'

'A sort of "seek and ye will not find"?'

'Well, yes, if you like.'

That was all I could get from him. He went back to wigs. He had done his bit for the Way.

The café wall was part of the main wall of the square, and of the sweeper's territory. She was near to us now. Her skin was shiny-tight, crinkling as she moved, like the skin on cold cocoa. Someone, trying to be kind, had injected ink above the middle joints of all her toes, and it had spread into smudged hawk-heads. She was as bent as a hairpin. She looked at her ankles. She swept like a metronome. She saw only our feet. I was a pair of scuffed brown boots. My friend had one foot on a chair, and so was a single slip-on Italian dress shoe, in fake crocodile. He threw a coin onto her strip. She picked it up in the course of one unbroken swing, dropped it wordlessly down her dress, and swept on. She did not look up.

I'd been unfair to the friend. I knew what he was talking about, but I wanted to taste again the salt humour of the undiscussable being discussed. That was the way I treated people and their ideas then. The humour was in this: insofar as one can talk sensibly about anything, the Eastern consensus would say, that thing is meaningless. For language itself is a silly illusion. So is reason, the child of language.

I'd been a Zen Buddhist, and knew well, and sympathised with, his distrust of the comprehensible. I knew the devices used to dislocate reasonable minds from the tramlines of logic so that, de-railed and free, they could seize the supra-reasonable. I'd studied koans and muttered mantras, and found in them some relief from the grind of linear thought. I found truth in the Eastern route, and moments of enlightenment. There was the resonance of paradox in many of the ironies taught smilingly by my Zen masters. But as I looked, there seemed only the slimmest of lines between irony and nonsense. There was also delusion, undiscovered by the selectively clear gaze of the yogi. I began to think that something was not necessarily true *because* it was paradoxical. And why discard reason altogether? The primacy of unreason in Zen thought seemed to me an arbitrary and suspiciously convenient choice. For reason has its own internal rules. Breach one and the others complain; a competent philosophical mechanic can hear the muttering, and correct. But in the land of unreason the rules of navigation are concocted by the individual explorer, or by the authority to whom he chooses to bow – authority which can't be questioned, because to question is to let in reason again through the metaphysical cat flap. Hence there's a highroad to exploitation, if one chooses a guide, or egotism if one charts one's own course.

The Self, said the Buddha, is the source of illusion, and its creature. Destroy it, and one has cleared away the scum on the lake of the world. Then one can see Reality, glittering sharply, with fabulous multifaceted beauty, at the bottom of all experience. 'Now I have found you,' said the Buddha, when he burst through into Enlightenment. 'Never again will you build the house of Self.' It's the language of triumphant soldiers confirming that they have located and eliminated a long-sought enemy.

Hinduism is less martial, more elusive, and more allusive. The illusion is that the Self *as a discrete unit* is real. Salvation consists in unity with Brahman, the real, cosmic Self; the mind whose thoughts not only authored and sustained the universe, but who *are* the Universe. Matter, mind and spirit appear to us to be distinct, but this appearance is illusory and catastrophic. 'All distinctions are falsely imagined,' said Hui-Neng. There's no neater summary of the Hindu doctrine of *advaita* – non-duality. To know this properly is to live it; to live it is to live properly. The Ego is the illusion of discrete existence and significance. 'The Absolute IS,' wrote Christmas Humphreys. 'We of the relative can neither add to it nor enter it nor take from it ought away. Yet we are part of it, we *are* it!' Hindus would prefer to talk about transcending the Ego, or putting it into its proper Brahmanic perspective, than about starving or bludgeoning it. But it perhaps comes to much the same thing; there's certainly a good deal of radical spiritual violence in the extreme asceticism of Hinduism.

Whatever language you use, there's a problem: the troops deployed in the East to assassinate the Ego are the fathers and the children of the Ego itself. It's not surprising that they don't do a thorough job. There are, of course, enigmatic poems to explain this away. I was intoxicated by their elegance for a while. But at last I thought that I needed an outside agent to do my selfishness to death. I thought that I had to revive the dogmatic dualism from which I'd run so long. I thought that it was necessary for a God who was not myself to adopt a strenuous interventionist policy. And I idolatrously worshipped that idea. The basic idea may have been right; its worship was not. Insofar as I had a creed, it was of denigration of everything that I feared and did not understand. The idol was finally smashed, along with a lot of my mind, many years after that trip to north India.

~

Sleep was elusive; I chased it and it wore me down. In the first part of the dark a nightjar gargled up and down its beat by my window. The gargle made my brain bitter. Light seeped out of holes in the shutters. Moths, drunk on it, wallowed in the light pools like boys in a summer waterfall. Brown moths shone. Everything shone in this night. The nightjar's mouth was like a trawl through the pools.

I had to keep on going up. Leeches had taken me to India. It doesn't matter why. I had a lot of paper already, covered with inky stamps and cryptic Hindi scrawls. But not quite enough.

I reached Tala in the dark. I was tired. Five hours next to the deputy assistant auditor of the Central Footwear Training Institute had aged me decades. A sack had burst as the bus lurched, filling my boots with lentils. A goat in the aisle licked some up, looked me hard in the eye, and belched in my face. I was grateful for the change of subject.

The road stopped at Tala, and I was alone in the bus as it rode the final circle around Queen Victoria and squeaked to a stop by some dripping pine trees. An old man in white pantaloons and a trilby hat sat by a pile of logs picking his nose. He rose as I approached him.

'Welcome. At your service. Where you from?'

'Thank you. England. Where does Dr Shankar live?'

'England good. Very good.' He placed his palms together. 'My brother went to England. To London. And Wolverhampton. He make very much money. Ice cream.'

'I'm glad. The English like ice cream. Where does Dr Shankar live?'

'His ice cream very good. Pistachio. Mango. In cardboard tubes. He has been to prison.'

'Where does Dr Shankar live?'

'He make thousands of tonnes. In all weathers. Green, blue, orange.'

I walked off. It had begun to rain. Dense clouds had blown

in, and I could see only a few yards. It felt like a cliff top; as if beyond the belt of trees there was only air and spindles of heavy cloud. A hand came at me through the fog, and the voice attached to it said, 'Strawberry. And vanilla.'

Twenty minutes later, when I'd broken free, a woman found me and took me silently to Shankar's house. It was a British bungalow in a clearing, at the top of a meandering lane of pine-needles. Roses clutched at my crotch. A gas lamp shaped like a blue-bell hissed in the porch. I thundered at the door. A woman's face peered through a porthole to one side, and a great unlocking began. Bolts, chains, keys galore. Then a pause. A bolt was scraped shut again and feet pattered away. Different feet returned, the unlocking continued. A very fat man oozed over the doorstep, his hand outstretched.

'You must be Dr Foster. We are honoured.'

I have never disliked anyone so immediately and so completely.

He took my hand and pulled me into the hall. He had damp, spongy palms. A vapour trail of scented soap marked his path. Mrs Shankar, the port-hole peeper, hovered by a rubber plant, alternately rubbing her knuckles in front of her and clasping her wrists behind her. Shankar made no reference to her.

'You've come far? Have you eaten?' He smiled solicitously.

'I've come from Delhi. And no, I haven't eaten.'

'Here. Eat.' He pointed to a bowl of sugared almonds on a cocktail table. 'And you can get breakfast in the morning *here.*' He jabbed with a swagger stick into a chart of the compound hanging next to a lithograph of Ganesh, the elephant-headed god.

'Thank you,' I murmured. 'Thank you.'

'Sit down. This is your home. Then we will go.' He grunted in Hindi. A sullen houseboy came. There were commands. The boy left and returned with an old black telephone on a very long lead. Shankar dialled, barked, and nodded at me. 'There may be a room in the lodge. Tomorrow the formalities.'

I bowed and left. It was not a good start. And it got no better.

~

*Chapter 3*

# PAUSING

'A monk came to the master, Nansen, and asked, "Is there some
teaching that no master has ever taught?"
"There is," said Nansen.
"Can you tell me what it is?" asked the monk.
Nansen said, "It is not Buddha. It is not things. It is not thinking."'

~

'Blow this for a lark, thought the small good wolf, so he said,
"All the better to eat with, my dear," and jumped out of bed to
get at the food in the basket. Little Red Riding Hood screamed,
and dropped it, and backed across the room...'

— Mary Raymer
*The Small Good Wolf*

~

## EDUCATION IN MYTH-MAKING: PART 1

'I am sorry, most sorry. It is not possible.'

I sat in Shankar's office the following morning. It was the
battleground for an unequal fight between deodorant and

sweat, rain and old British windows, mould and old British journals, sense and nonsense. A piece of paper was missing, and this was apparently fatal to my research proposals.

'You need a yellow permit.'

'Can I have one, please? You are a very important man. I'm sure that you can arrange it.'

He swelled dangerously and spoke for the first time with real regret. 'No, not even I can do it. You must go to Delhi.'

'I've just come from Delhi. They told me there that I had everything I needed. I went to four government departments and seven sub-departments. Why was I not told about this?'

He shrugged. 'We must go through the Right Channels.'

I despised the capital letters. 'My sponsors (and I dropped the name of an important scientific society) will be very unhappy.' I paused. I looked up at an eagle tearing off a squirrel's head, and watched dark moons of sweat rise under Shankar's arms. I continued. 'With you.'

'With me?' Shankar's jowls shuddered. His palms came up from his knees and spread stickily out on a mountainous in-tray. A monkey skull lay on his desk – a paperweight, like so much else in India. He picked it up, rolled it in his hands, stared into its sockets and chattered its jaws together as if consulting it. He heaved, shut his eyes and flowed deeper into the chair. He had been at the temple that morning. The red dye on his forehead had streamed in his sweat down the bridge of his nose. Scarlet beads clustered like holly berries round the stiff hairs on the tip. When he spoke again it was with an ancient, implacable exhaustion. His eyes opened first, and I could almost hear them creaking. He was a brontosaurus, rearing his head from a hot swamp. He chewed silently on nothing for a moment, and then: 'Form D151 is mandatory for all personnel working with whole organisms. A leech is a whole animal. So is a cow. And so is a rabbit.' He delivered this Buddha-like, as if he were saying, 'A rabbit is a whole animal. This is the incontrovertible wisdom of the East.' I loathed this man.

It was time for an iconoclastic change of tactic. I got up and shut the door to the brontosaurus's byre. I looked conspiratorially around, as if I expected spies behind the filing cabinets. I sat down again, pulling my chair closer to the desk.

'We are a long way from Delhi. We are high in the hills. This is your empire. You are the boss. Why should a clerk many days down a muddy road tell you, Dr Shankar, PhD, what you should or should not allow in your own home?'

He looked puzzled, then pleased, as if the sweet young taste of insurrection was creeping over his tongue for the first time. The boy, Shankar, had plainly never put a drawing pin on his teacher's chair. Now, to his credit, it seemed as if part of him was regretting it; was wondering if it was not too late to make amends for fifty years of blameless conformity. I hoped that that, mixed with my ridiculous assertions of his omnipotence, would prove a heady cocktail. I donned my red tights and danced demonically before him.

'You are a scientist of distinction,' I lied. 'I know that

you'd never let the silly men in suits stand in the way of the quest for truth.' I wondered if I was over-egging this already pretty sickly pudding, but saw no signs of it in Shankar's damp and wobbly face. 'And just think how impressed your staff will be by this gesture of independence.'

The cheeks tightened. The mist blew out of his eyes. I'd gone too far. I should have guessed that the camp would be full of stiletto-wielding informers waiting for Shankar to make a bureaucratic slip; waiting to knock him off the tree so that they could climb up. I'd forgotten that Indian science was a career; that forms and reports were the bulwark of the status quo; that to be successful was to be an administrator of the real work and the real thoughts of others. If it's right that Indians live naturally in the unconscious, it's also true that they leave it more determinedly and thoroughly than anyone else. They seem less capable of living amphibiously in both camps. Perhaps this is a compliment – I'm not yet sure. An Indian administrator is more thoroughly and irredeemably enthralled by the immediate and the material than any New Jersey real estate agent.

Shankar wallowed briskly in his chair, shaking off the remaining threads of the spell.

'That is quite impossible.' He touched a bell. 'You must go to Delhi.'

No, I thought right away. No. And the next day some good news arrived. The road had dissolved in the rain and slid off the mountain. For the moment, at least, I had to stay where I was.

I went three times a day through hot red rain, through trees that smelt of mice and gravy, through walls of faces and past the odd demon, through dripping rhododendrons that reminded me of a Scottish keeper's daughter called Kirsty, past a Hornbill's nest, to the temple. I sat outside on a wet stone, under my umbrella, and watched. I don't know and didn't know then what I was watching for, but it seemed important not to miss whatever it was.

The hill water took the same route to the temple. Sometimes the people waded ankle deep to their god. The god was Vishnu, the ineffable, borne on an eagle, without beginning or end, from whom all things emanate; incarnated twenty-four times, including as a fish, a turtle, a man-lion, a dwarf, a swan and the Buddha. From his navel sprang a lotus, and from the lotus sprang Brahma, and from Brahma sprang the Universe. Vishnu has many arms but often only four are shown. In one hand he holds a wheel, signifying the Universal mind and the cycle of creation and annihilation; in one he holds a conch shell, signifying purity, honesty, righteousness and salvation; in one he holds a mace, indicating the power of enlightenment and knowledge; the final hand holds a lotus, a symbol of majesty and earth. Inside the temple he lay in the near-dark, light from a butter-lamp flickering over his golden face, reclining on the coils of the multi-headed serpent-king, Sesanaga. The people brought him all they could afford, and often more than they could afford.

And I sat outside, waiting for something. I was a boy, and the boy thought it was childish to have many arms, or the trunk of an elephant, or many heads, and despised the gaudiness of the temple – indeed despised anything that was really colourful. Instead of being impressed by the immense complexity of Hindu belief – in which every cadence of existence has a precise mythological corollary – I was oppressed by it, as indeed by every other appearance of complexity in the world – and ran scared from it into formulae and propositions of laughable simplicity. But it is perhaps something that I sat there.

Jagjit was a Sikh. I liked him. He was very good at fishermen's knots, but hopeless at tying his turban. It didn't peak neatly out from his forehead, but boiled up and over. I met him in Nainital, where I had been to eat cake, bleach a bat's skull and hope for a letter. He was running for a bus. His turban unravelled like a pig being disembowelled, snared his pounding legs, and sent him spread-eagled under a bicycle. He picked himself up and bolted for the bus. As the bus pulled away, he was still hauling in the cloth, hand over hand through the door, his etiolated hair limp and crimped around his shoulders, tyre marks across his face, laughing away the pain. I clamped his bleeding nose with a page ripped from my notebook, and we were friends. He vomited as tidily as any duchess as we lurched round the bends into the clouds.

His father, a dairy farmer in the Punjab, sent him parcels of cheese every fortnight. I got to know Jagjit because he loathed cheese. He couldn't touch it. It made him ill. But he couldn't bring himself to tell his father, for fear of hurting his feelings. So Jagjit solemnly thanked his father, and stockpiled the cheese. He had a small bungalow, facing north towards the snow. There was cheese everywhere. He used it for bookends, and as a stand for his electric organ. He asked me if I liked the stuff, and I slowly eroded the cheese mountain. One day I was sitting at the kitchen table eating a door-stop, and Jagjit watched me, amused. Then he asked, 'Do you like India?' There was no hyperbole about Jagjit.

'It's very interesting.'

He blew down his nose in a sort of laugh. 'It's taken a while, but we've learned what that means.'

'What's that?'

'That you see the dirt.'

'I see other things too.'

'Perhaps you do. The Taj Mahal, maybe, or the ghosts at Varanasi.' He was goading me. 'What else is there?'

He had a small brass barrel of orange juice in the corner of the room. He got up, filled a tankard with it, and sat down. 'In-di-a,' he said slowly, picking out the three syllables, 'is a vast, wild temple where unconsciousness is consciously worshipped.'

I knew he'd go on if I said nothing.

'This awe of sleep, of passivity, of the passion-free life, is awe of a second-generation god. The first god, its father, was Paradox. And India loved and worshipped him. Surely you can understand India's love of Paradox? Paradox is elegant, and moves well, and has spice on his lips. But the love became debased. It spawned an ugly child, called Contradiction. Contradiction looks like Paradox, as you'd expect. But it's a bastard child, conceived during a million illicit nights in Bihar and Uttar Pradesh. But India loved her child. Doted on it. Told it the old stories of India, and fed it the sweetmeats of Mumbai. And it grew on these things. Grew fat, reclining in the family home. And then it spoke with a voice all its own. And India, delighted, listened, and was convinced.'

Jagjit stopped and smiled a little, looking embarrassed. I asked him if he was. He said that he was not. They were not his words, but the sermon of an uncle who had written many books and painted many pictures. The uncle had been in prison for years, and so could see things clearly.

'Go on,' I said, but he seemed to be finished. He did continue, though, as if starting a new story.

'Contradiction said puerile things that the rest of the world had grown out of. But India believed them. It believed that you had to be asleep in order to be awake; had to be black to be white; had to be dead to be alive. To the people in the villages this sounded like the old real wisdom of paradox. In fact it was nonsense. It opened the way to grand, basic lies. To the lie that you had to be false in order to be true. For a thousand years there was an orgy of relativism. But the relativism was not complete. If it had been, it wouldn't have been so sinister. There was an Absolute, and it was the Self − enthroned, apparently, in order to destroy it. But it got comfortable on its throne, and couldn't be displaced. So the great Eastern orgy was not a festival of consummation, not a celebration that the Indian soul had finally achieved union with the otherness of the Universe, as it proclaimed.

But rather a long evening of masturbation. We welcomed ourselves as the one and only god, for ever and ever, Amen.'

This was strange talk from a Sikh with a house of cheese. It was the last I could draw from him. In some ways this was a shame. He spoke well. He libelled India horribly, but that's what I wanted to hear. It confirmed the position into which I'd argued myself, and from which I was too fearful to move. At one level, I believed him for a couple of decades. He has a lot to answer for.

He could run better than he could philosophise. I learned this three miles up a goat track which wound round and up a terraced hill on the north edge of the encampment. We stood one evening on his balcony, spitting cornflakes into the clouds. Jagjit pointed out Panchuli, which he always did, and we were silent, as we always were. Then he said, 'See, I'll race you along that path.' He pointed across the valley, past a cluster of huts and a tangle of bracken, to an unterraced hillside. It would be a happy scramble up and a happy tumble down. My legs normally did what they were told. Jagjit was a twig-legged, sparrow-chested stool-percher, who liked cricket statistics. But he had issued the challenge. 'Of course,' I said. 'Prepare for humiliation.'

Jagjit was wearing his usual early evening pyjamas and his feet were bare. It was plainly no contest. And, for a while, it wasn't. I bounded down into the valley bottom, forded the river and started strongly up the first slope, pulling away from Jagjit with every stride. It was easy enough. The mud was hard. Looking back as I turned the corner of the hill, I saw Jagjit just out of the river and stumbling up the bank, parting the goats as he went through them, like a comb in a head of mottled hair. We were high here, and I wondered how my Cambridge lungs would fare in the thin air that Jagjit had breathed for years. But there seemed no need to worry. Round the corner the path angled down slightly through a field of scrub grass. There were no settlements on this side, just a meshwork of dry-stone goat folds by the river that churned and curdled in foaming pots. We were running to a path-side cairn on a cruelly false summit. Go past a white-washed temple, Jagjit had said, then through a meadow of yellow alpine flowers, and there will be half a mile to go. I could see neither, but I was running well, loosening all the time, and the cold air was splashing my face. Through a patch of gravel I went, kicking chippings into the grass, thinking guiltily of Jagjit's feet. The path wound tightly on itself. I couldn't see what it did a hundred yards ahead. I expected the gentle climb to continue.

When I turned the corner, the path wasn't there. Or rather not in the direction it had been. It turned sharply left. The hill sprang straight into the sky. Jagjit's temple wobbled on a bracket bolted into the rock. Way beyond it was the cairn. A wide shallow sheet of brown floodwater slid past it, collecting and speeding in a narrow stone funnel. Out of this funnel, the steam fell fifty feet clear of the hillside, smashing as it hit the wide ledge below, throwing up a silver ribbon of spray, which smashed the evening light in turn, painting a broad border of fire.

At first the path was cinder dry. I thought that would help, but it was scattered with bone hard goat pellets, like green ball-bearings. I scrabbled and bled. Further on I braced myself against the hill again, leant into it, and felt the stress in my calves, hard from the heather moors of Yorkshire. I fought on. Then I hit the poor air like a wall. It was as if a vein had been opened; that I was flowing out into the goat shit. Giddiness fluttered over me; my diaphragm creaked; the world closed in. I couldn't stop running; I'd never have restarted the pistons.

Jagjit caught me at the foot of the slate pitch. A goat's head was nailed to a post. Thorns had been driven into its eyes. Jagjit grinned, slapped me on the back and said, 'Chant the *om mani padme hum* in time with your strides. It will help. Then your feet will become a mantra and you'll float up, like a prayer.' It was odd advice from an orthodox Sikh. Later he said that there were particular religious horses for particular religious courses, and that he was always a Tantrist in the mountains.

He didn't stop. His feet rolled out as they hit the ground, like a sailor's on a rocking deck. He rolled up, sending trickles of gravel muttering back. He loped past the temple, pausing to kiss a monk's knee stump. I buffeted on. Sweat filled and stung my eyes. He was waiting for me at the top.

'You're okay?'

'Fine,' I lied. 'On you go.'

This released him. He ran with great joy. This was wild and fine.

He didn't patronise when I panted in through the door. He had changed, and trimmed his beard. He nodded and smiled. 'It's a pretty hill,' he said.

It was. Just here India stretches up and looks over into Tibet. At the edge of vision, like eyelashes, are dusty trees full of coloured birds. Then the hills clamber up, biting scallops out of the cloud. In monsoon time, the cloud is mostly sallow over the peaks. But in the early morning the sky wakes in a gusty fuss, sucks the clouds up to the sun, and spits snow into the mountain basins.

I wrote down the story of the run immediately afterwards because I thought it was significant, that it said something about joy. Now I don't know if it indicates anything or not, but I do know that only sad bores see parables wherever they look.

In a room in Cambridge, I'd learned to count from one to nine and back again, yanking my mind back whenever it wandered to somewhere I'd not told it to go. It had never once occurred to me to ask who this 'I' was that was doing the yanking.

The road wouldn't be impassable forever. Shankar was still insistent. To Delhi I must go. And there I'd have to hawk myself around a dozen dozy departments – to watch my applications being skewered on in-spikes on a hundred desks; to ring bells and demand to see the superiors of a thousand clerks with bovine eyes; to listen to the cud-chewing of filing secretaries; to interpret the clatter of moribund typewriters; to learn the bizarre ecology of Indian offices, where the niches are the immutable boundaries of status and responsibility and privilege drawn by the sovereign statute of custom. No, I thought again; no.

Then the amoebae moved into my small intestine and solved the problem. I was spectacularly ill – on an involuntary hunger strike against Indian bureaucracy. The flesh slid off me, like the road had slipped off the mountain. Shankar was terrified, which made it all pure pleasure. The paperwork involved in a European death must be horrific. The face that sneered up at him when he came on his gushingly solicitous visits was sunk and pallid. A bubbling bronchitis came in on top and stole my sleep. I mopped my armpits with newspaper, strained over a long drop, read Dickens (*ex libris* Captain Barnabas Fitzpatrick), and ate pickled eggs. And outside the rains came.

All the water in the world was here. There was a glorious week of fever, when the cough ripped up the nights, and snakes spat into my eyes. I slept in my clothes under a single blanket. There was always rain, hammering on the tiles, rapping on the doors, dancing down the glass and gurgling down the cast iron gutters.

The rain never shone. North India is always grey in my head, which is a terrible thing to say about my head.

I didn't care how fast or how slowly time passed. I was puzzled by that neutrality. I was mildly happy when the night came, for that meant that another day had been notched up, and somehow that seemed to be a good thing. I was glad to see mornings, because they were mornings. It was perfect monasticism, and therefore very imperfect human being. I was on my own for thousands of hours a day, and when I wasn't, I was on my own but with someone else in the room. It was cold. Fog barred the sight beyond a few yards from the window. But I had a blanket, books, paper, and the conceit that I had something to say. I waited for homesickness to burst over me and crush out little things and usher in a new force and clarity of thought. It never came. When I thought of England, it was distorted so as to be unrecognisable by sentiment, and beyond the reach of desire. A., for instance. She is very beautiful. But she always wandered through my head with monstrously elongated feet. The Yorkshire tree in which I sat every night, watching the heather moor, became a bundle of sticks. The grey walls of racing, roaring water that bowled me screaming into the beaches were mute and low. The singing skies of Somerset were still, and no one came out with me into the woods at the edge of the night. The old tunes in my mind were just old; no patina. So I gave up on A., and trees, and surf, and England. I also gave up hoping that I'd be able to write anything shrewd about India. I couldn't empathise, and so lacked the compassion which is the prerequisite of real sight.

I went out into the dusk to look over the cloud forest. To watch for something. A wide table of rock, spread beneath an arbour of firs, jutted over the top of the tree canopy two hundred feet below. There were pockmarks of hut-light on the face of the night. You could creep down a gully in the rock and stand astride a crack which split the whole table from top to bottom, and have nothing but air in every direction except under your boot soles. But tonight I was on the top, weak and blinking. A figure moved by the rock and spoke softly in an old language. A shadow under the overhang deepened as two figures joined it. It seemed to me, leaning against a tree, my face tickled by leaves, that the air was full of bone dust, although the rain had washed the wind. The sentinel by the rock hardened out of the dust as I watched. A boy sang. India murmured. It always murmurs.

I read 'Pickwick' by the light of a thin candle stuck to the bottom of an upturned ashtray by a wild root system of wax. Because I was young, I was happier with a candle. It made me think I was living. Things seemed deeper and cleaner — the monkey's foot on the shelf; the water bottle with its strap hanging in a loop like a bridle; the umbrella with an embroidered handle leaning against the table where the rest of my life happened; books, notebooks, pens, and pills. Across in the cupboard, a bag of old mangoes rustled as the maggots worked. In the trembling light, the relationships between these things became closer and more obvious, and seemed intentional. In unblinking electricity they merely had surfaces, and the mangoes were only coincidentally near to the shrew trap. Now they had a new significance; each was defined by its relationship to all the others.

It got colder. More blankets arrived. I smelt them before deciding how I'd lay them on the bed — the cleanest next to me, the next cleanest on top, and the worst sandwiched in between.

Very early one thunderous morning, when the sky was splitting over the plains, my myth making began in earnest. The gardener stamped muddily down the corridor and kicked at my door. I opened up.

'Yes?'

He looked hard at me. I was stupid not to understand.

'Sahib?'

'What's the matter?'

He wrung his hands. Books say that stressed people wring their hands. Usually they don't. But in India they do, and the gardener really did.

'Cows. Flowers.'

'What are you talking about?'

I hardly knew this man. I had nodded at him as he mooched around, and once he had beckoned me urgently, and showed me his earwig trap behind the potting shed. I was grateful, of course, but it was a flimsy foundation for friendship. The tea boy had said that he was 'very bad man. Oh, with such a very black heart. He gets drunkest, and then, oh dear, he goes smash, smash, smash.'

Now he stood jumpily at the door, pyjamas flapping in the wind from China. Cows had wandered through his rose beds, trampling them to clay. One cow ate some thorns, got colicky, and dribbled blood. Only the gardener minded about the roses, but the villagers were worried about the cow. Fearful that it might bring catastrophically bad luck on them all. The gardener had been cold-shouldered, and children had stoned him when he'd gone to get his milk. They had spat out a couple of martial verses from the Mahabharata, and chalked a pentacle on his rabbit hutch.

What, I wondered, did he want me to do about it?

'Write a letter.'

'To whom? Saying what?'

He wouldn't come into the room. Behind him, the wide eyes of the inevitable spectators moved as one as each actor spoke.

The gardener began. From what I could gather from his mime, his cryptic similes and the corrections and caveats of the audience, a man had skidded his motorcycle into a Brahmin cow ('it have hump, like the postman') somewhere near Kolkata ('where the trees have hair, and the river has babies'). Eventually the cow had died ('it go twitch, twitch, all day, like a fern'). The rider had been tied to a post in the sun to watch, and when the cow twitched its last ('it give a huge wail, and the people all cry') the villagers rolled the man over the edge of a disused quarry. They would have stoned him to death had a star not risen. No one recognised the star, and so it was taken to be the cow, happy and released, eschewing vengeance.

I did not believe the tale.

'But Sahib, it was in the newspaper.'

There was a collective nod.

'So what do you want me to do?'

'Write a letter.'

'Why? To whom?'

'Is it too much? Write a letter.'

The gardener stepped inside the room, pushing me aside, pulled out a pad of paper from my desk and slammed a pencil on top.

'Write, Sahib. You must.'

No one could tell me what should be in the letter, or to whom it should go. So I sat down, the company flooded around, and I wrote out Henry V's speech to his men before Agincourt, addressed it 'Dear Sir' and promised I would post it.

The gardener beamed and bowed. The painter slapped the gardener on the back and shook my hand twice. The others smiled and backed out of the room. Everyone was happy.

Next day, propped against the dahlias in a jam jar on my bedside table, was a post card of an improbably buxom Bollywood star. 'To my deer frend,' it said, in careful capitals. 'From Hariprasad. I did not die last nite.'

I was still ill. The fever boiled in my temples. But there was sometimes quiet in the night, and sometimes I forgot my bowels and my bronchi. People scampered in and out of the room. Some brought gifts – apples; flowers; a stone with the Union Jack scraped into it; a mute bulbul which scratched out its own eyes and was dead the day after it arrived, one foot still clutching the obituaries from the *Deccan Chronicle*.

Some brought propriety, stiff bows, awkward silences, and salaams: 'We thought it our duty to come, to wish you the best blessings.'

Jagjit came, read some short stories by Somerset Maugham, and looked wan.

'I think of palm trees,' he said, 'and of course I am sad.'

Outside, to make the langurs run, the gardeners just stood and guffawed at them.

Often, too, the tea-boy came, knocking nervously and waiting to see that the tea was good before backing out again. He brought the little commonplaces that passed as news. 'The grass is green today, Sahib.' 'A tree fell near the water tank.' 'Tomorrow Bismillah may scrub the balcony.' 'The postman is to be married to the daughter of the goat-butcher. She has a wrinkle in her leg, but she is a good cook and has many buffaloes.' One day, casually, he dropped some devastating words. 'The road is open, Sahib. They use biggest bulldozers.'

The plan was quickly made. I would remain ill. Shankar's movements were wholly predictable. In the day, I'd get the leeches I needed, and do my work on them at night. I'd like to be able to say that the leech hunt was a motif of colossal metaphorical power, like Peter Matthiessen's Zen hunt for the Snow Leopard. But it would be a lie. I did my leeches, and I did my spiritual cogitation, and neither taught me much about the other.

Jagjit was a fine accomplice. His eyes shone when I told him about the idea. The guards were poor. Twenty rupees would be enough. He danced off to fix it, a happy schoolboy with a blueprint for a vast and diabolical paper dart.

I was the leech bait. The cattle pools heaved with them. When Shankar was dozing in his swamp, I slank down to the farm, rolled up my trouser legs, and stood in the shallows. I splashed around for a while, for agitated water attracts leeches, and soon began to feel the itches that tell that there's a leech on the skin. These were big, rubbery cattle leeches, stretching to five inches on full extension, and they moved in the water with a beautiful oscillating serpentine motion. The pool was clear enough, and I could see what they were doing. They swam up beside my legs, drawn by the amino acids swilling off the skin, and by the disturbance and the warmth. Then they paused on stones a few inches away, attached by their rear suckers, wavering, questing and undulating. Then there was a sudden moment of decision; the head lunged and the rear sucker detached, and the leech muddled through the water and attached to the leg. The head quested a bit more, snuggling around close to the skin, and then buried down in it, injecting its local anaesthetic and its anticoagulant and started to feed. It was beautiful.

Sometimes I let them feed, for it is a wonderful thing to see those black segmented bodies with the pairs of yellow eyes arranged along the back swell fast as the blood is pumped into the caecal pouches in the gut. But really I needed hungry leeches, and so, before feeding began, I usually lifted my leg out of the pond, dabbed a spot of surgical spirit on them to make them let go, and popped them in the collection jar. I'd get fifty in a good afternoon.

It was important to get several species of leech. The terrestrial ones were common in the monsoon. They were easy to find and to catch, for they found and caught me. It was best to walk noisily, behind a companion, through undergrowth or paths used by goats, sheep or men. The front man was rarely attacked, but his presence alerted dozy leeches to a nearby feed. They sprang to attention, standing upright on their rear suckers, bodies rippling and seeking, ready for the man behind. They dropped from trees too, which was a menace. After each hunt we stripped off and checked each other's backs for leeches. It was also wise to search your crotch. The Americans in Vietnam, terrified of what they euphemised as 'Urethral hirundiasis', issued condoms to their troops, not for the bordellos of Saigon, but to be worn when wading through swamps or trekking through leech-rich areas.

The local children joined in. The rate was one rupee for ten leeches, and my leech-collecting lesson has now appeared on the CV of at least one university-educated engineer. Leeches bit better in the mornings, said the children, but they'd try whenever they could. They brought me five hundred, but many were damaged. The children typically left them to feed for too long, and pulled them too hard, leaving the head in the wound. That wasn't good for the leech, the child, or me.

The farm workers helped by driving the cattle into the water. Huge numbers of leeches clustered around the prominent milk vein and the udder, and many stayed on after the cattle lumbered out of the water. Everyone thought I was mad, of course, but they humoured me cheerily, and thought it a good game. Sometimes they'd squint at me and say with tilted head:

'Why, Sahib, why?'

'Science,' I would reply. 'Very important.'

And they rejoined, quite rightly, 'Why?'

I didn't know. I still don't.

Shankar went home at five precisely, sauntered round a loop of forest between six and twenty-five past, shouting at his dog when it ran after the monkeys, and sat on a bench at the head of the valley, looking towards the north. He smoked two pipes of Danish duty-free tobacco, knocking them out against the bole of a tree which was black where his ash had soaked into the grain. Then he sighed, and walked back, kicking the sand of the track for the first two hundred yards, then straightening up and bustling to his bungalow. He scraped his feet on an iron gnome by the doorstep, shouted for the boy, and went inside. I know this because for a week I watched it all, crouched in Kirsty's rhododendrons.

Inside, he washed his hands with scented soap, dabbed his ears with cologne from a green glass bottle by the sink, and sank onto a cracked leather sofa to play snakes and ladders with an imaginary friend. At eight he rang a bell on a cocktail table, and the boy arrived to report on the state of the dinner. Dinner was at quarter past, in silence; Shankar at one end of a long, feudal table, inlaid with hickory elephants; his wife at the other, her watery eyes turned down on the elephants. Dinner ended with a belch. He read pornography until ten. She embroidered. They both ate chocolates. Then the magazine was replaced neatly in its pile, and the row tied off. Then bed. I know this because for three nights I saw it all, prowling in the shrubbery by the lace curtains, before going to do things to leeches by candlelight, watched by dead Englishmen in wing collars and bowties.

Every afternoon I went to a chai house at the brow of the hill, overlooking the village. It was one of the more respectable places, with a wooden roof rather than a tin one, so you could still talk when it was raining, and a proper oak table with 'Corporal Bush: RIP' carved into one leg. The place hung over the valley; the hill slid towards it. I always sat in the corner (for stateless, dispossessed men are particularly territorial) with a brass bird-cage full of hens' eggs. At my right elbow, a wall of cloud squeezed between some woolly trees (they should have been blasted, but this isn't a properly poetic book) and a black ridge which lurched into the air and dropped back into the valley with a stomach-churning jolt as the eye traced it.

The road itself was a fine story. The chai-house was a drain for the human watershed of the road. Traffic sluiced up and down. Children skipped, stared at and stoned the monkeys; old men in khaki serge jerkins and forage caps, with eyes that pretended to stare through and not at, walked up stiffly (for they'd bend otherwise), with their umbrellas hooked onto their back collars. And women, fatter, cheaper and confident. They were banded, pendanted, pierced and scented jackdaws, jangling along the great road – tight-wrapped if young, or else in flowing swathes to hide the age, the stumbles and the bulging. The older women wore cardigans with plastic buttons which wouldn't meet. However big the dogs were, they skittered like little dogs, and showed too much white in their eyes.

They marched stiffly and lolled – looking martial, looking shy, moustaches bristling, pigtails swinging, umbrellas cradled, babies straggling, braced proud as crows, twittering like sparrows. They came with sacks on their shoulders, bags on their arms, bent and stumbling; the face the same whether the job was crippling or fun. Past stalls hanging in the cloud, and dark inside with the talk of old men remembering the other days when they'd sat there and remembered. Past the shoe-maker doubly untouchable from the leather and the dust, crouched in a pile of soles. Past the shed where I bought a goat leg with a tattoo from the newspaper it had been wrapped in, telling of a woman in Madhya Pradesh whose child had been born with an elephant's head. Past the school where the children were brushed until they shone; where they learned how to calculate the speed of sound, and why bodies are burned at Varanasi. Past the trees where the langurs whooped and crashed, and past the cache of stones for pelting them. And then, having passed all these things, the people went in a thousand directions, fanning along the lacy goat-tracks like streams in a great delta. Down to the wood where the woodpeckers drummed, and up to the cliff where the lammergeier rode the air-surf. To little moss-covered lean-tos which throbbed when the rains came. To sedate bungalows with kitchen gardens, made to remind sergeant majors of Kent.

I was on a ridge between two immensely deep valleys that cut north and south, slashing on into the plains, and on into Tibet. Every afternoon they filled with mist, like pots boiling over. At noon the fog-curd crusted the lowest Tala goat path. Then it bubbled up, filling the minds of the people who dreamt in the shacks and snored in the bungalows.

I came to have tea above the clouds every afternoon at four. And all the time I wondered when I would meet India. I'd met stories – Shankar, Jagjit and a cow that became a star. But I had been cheated of India.

Walking alone in the pines, I climbed a tree to peer into a nest, came down, and, tired by the effort, fell onto a bed of bracken and slipped happily into unconsciousness with crickets whirring and the sun hot on my face. I must have been there for an hour or so; there was time to dream of waves crashing on a northern shore and limpets, weak with clinging, crawling up a jetty for cover. A kittiwake tilted a wing in some cold sun, and a shoal of sand eels wriggled at the back of my eye. Then there were snatches of dream drifting between me and India for a while, and then an un-marine rustling which punched me awake in a flurry of suspicion. A woman stood in the clearing. She was young. Probably she was pretty. She looked half amused and half outraged. She took an apple from a bag tied loosely round her, crossed to me and put it down at my feet. She laughed, like water falling, and ran fast and hard down the path.

I sat, throwing out the thoughts as I'd been taught, and again, never wondering who was throwing them out.

For long periods I spoke to no one, and almost forgot how. This is common in lone travellers. When I had to speak, there was a strained mute moment, like air being blown across a stopped organ pipe, before any noise came. Once launched, sentences usually sailed well enough, but starting new phrases was an effort. So, to avoid the danger of a stammering break, I tried not to punctuate. Breathing was the worst casualty. Like everyone else, I've learned to make my breath last for the phrase being spoken, and to take breath at natural punctuation points, points worked out with an eye to the substance of the talk. This requires a good deal of forethought. You need to have an idea how the phrases will fall. That pacing skill was lost quickly in the silence. I was a funny, inarticulate creature, who'd take deep breaths, run hard at sentences and lose momentum, ending in a squeaky decrescendo of embarrassed despair.

Aloneness has other side effects. When you are alone you can buy facts without using the debased currency of second-hand perceptions or presumptions, and so you get better value from the world. But it's not all good. There's the arrogant dogmatism of thoughts unchecked by the usefully dismissive laughter of others. I became sure, for instance, sure beyond doubt, that Indian flies, unlike English ones, remember the way out when they fly into a room.

There's no question, though, that aloneness is a fine tool for exposing the multifacetedness of things: you simply have more time to turn over and over the toys we call facts. You can see how they glitter in the light of quiet. But aloneness is hopeless for discovering new facts. In aloneness, without external boundary markers, the Self quickly asserts itself as the absolute. And here is where we start getting religious again. The 'facts' uncovered by the light of the 'absolute self' are narcissistic delusions. The lonely cross-legged men in a *za-zen* trance aren't doing the ego to death, as they hope, but rather worshipping it in a new language. The language of their devotion is so obscure, so alien to the common idea of selfhood, that the men think that it can't be addressed to the Ego. But the Ego is clever, multi-lingual, and catholic in its tastes. It is happy to receive compliments in all tongues. It can feed off many foods, and grow secretly grotesque.

'Hmm,' said Jagjit, when I said this to him. 'Perhaps. Jung and Augustine, eh? Strange bedfellows.'

Later, in Nepal, a Rinpoche grinned, 'You don't know about the Void: find out. Then get to know the Void. Then get to be the Void. Then you will know.'

In a sudden explosion of light, in the air over the trees, a pair of swifts screamed for a long moment, and seemed for that moment to be stuck to the sky – unchanging in every detail, but moving as fast as ever before; immutable, but without the stiffness of a silhouette; lent a new fluidity by the fact of unchangeableness. Then a gust nudged a cloud on and the light was gone; the swifts angled and dived below the parapet of a farm. I knew then, as Peter Matthiessen put it, that 'all names fall short of the shining of things', but this was an old lesson, re-learned. That patch of sky over India had a musty, homely smell, like an old exercise book. It should have had inkblots and spelling corrections.

The mountain people of North India are sturdy, dark and garrulous and see their world obliquely, as if the flat places tilt. It is difficult for an Englishman to get to this vantage point, and so the English use words like 'subtle', 'stoic', 'patient' or 'inscrutable'. The really remarkable thing about these Indians is a sort of conversational holism — every sentence operates at several different levels. I started off thinking that this was incoherence. I slowly came to know that that was precisely what it was not.

'Tonight you eat with me in my house, Sahib, but Durbar, please, Sahib, he must not know and I insult you by mentioning it, but he must not know, and we have meat, for rice is not good at night, for rice is cold and makes a man's insides all cold, O yes, and death will creep up faster.'

'I think that Subta is stealing my chickens, for many are gone, and he looks fat, but he is my friend, and so I care for him, especially since he will not have peace for a very long time, because he steals chickens, and it's not nice not to have peace.'

These people were kind to me. They fed me, brought me flowers and leeches, and leapt giggling out of the bushes to make me jump. Jagjit translated their stories around the tea kettle in their huts at night. The talk went on until the last listener fell asleep, and I slept well, on straw-stuffed cushions alive with fleas. I wrote the stories down at dawn as the children rubbed their eyes, ran out to drive the goats onto the hill and ran back to ask me for rupees or biros when their fathers could not hear.

So I gathered many strands, then went up high and tried to see a pattern, and slowly I began to know how these lives were woven. If an integrated personality means no partitions, these were very whole people. They did not distinguish between myth and the mundane. Ram told of the snakes crawling on the head of Shiva in the same tone as he spoke of the cobra which bit his aunt last spring by the rushes. But it wasn't, quite, that he was familiar and matter-of-fact about the supernatural; nor that he saw the littlenesses of his own life as part of a grand epic. Both Shiva and the cobra had the same quality of immanence; he was merely in a place where he could note that they did.

They knew no boundary between the objective and the subjective. They didn't 'think' something – they asserted it. They didn't 'feel good today' – they *were* good. There were no future intentions, and certainly no contingencies – there were certainties. This was easy, of course, in a world where little happened that was within human control. Each day was the same, bar the weather. Only a world busier than the Garwhal Himal faces real speculation about whether one's own perceptions of things are correct. Pulling on a crumpled roll of marijuana in Varanasi, a sadhu said: 'The truth is within you. Everything you search for is there. It's your own obsession with the "I" which blocks your view of those truths. Why do you look outside?'

'I'm confused,' I said. 'I look outside because that's the only way I can rid myself of the obsession with the "I" you say is so dangerous. Yet you tell me to look *in*, and so to see.'

'Work at it,' the sadhu said. 'Work at it.'

## EDUCATION IN MYTH-MAKING: PART 2

Vilayat introduced me to a man who knew about maize. I don't know why. I have no interest in maize. As soon as I shook the man's hand he started to talk about his grandfather.

When the grandfather was a small boy, he had been taken out to shoot a buffalo-killing tiger. This was in a tiny wizened village seven miles north of us. The grandfather was the gun-bearer, and he'd polished the gun (a black powder muzzle-loader, said to have killed in the Mutiny) with fine wool, plucked from the underside of a sheep's jaw and dipped in a jelly-soap made by boiling hare's bones. The jelly made the barrels gleam, and because it was from hares, made the bullets fly fast.

The grandfather and his father sat in a tree near a recent kill for five nights. For three nights they heard and saw nothing but an owl which made a clucking pass at the grandfather's head. They both caught colds. On the fourth night there was a low throb like the distant engine of a big ship, and the gentle parting of grass, and a barking scream as a muntjac was cuffed in the head and tossed. In the morning there was a dribble of blood on crushed bracken, and four-dimpled pads the size of dinner plates. They lost the spoor on the scree, and had to come back for the fifth night.

The evening started badly. A chicken was killed for supper, and the mother, rummaging through the guts, found that it had two stomachs. In one was a 500 *parsi* coin; in the other the heart-shaped seed case of a forest poppy. The augurer was called. He muttered for a while and confessed himself baffled. Such bafflement was bad. Good was always comprehensible.

When the chicken was eaten it tasted of fish. This too meant nothing obvious, and so was bad.

Then the two went out towards the place of the last kill. They climbed a tree, and it was so comfortable that the great-grandfather reminded the grandfather that he must be careful to stay awake. The spirits easily invade men who sleep in trees.

The tree was high above the ground wind, and they knew that their stink wouldn't trickle down into the grass. They watched the sun sink. The grandfather said he could see the world turning. The cold stiffened their trigger fingers, and chilled the cicadas shut. The dark was not complete. Orion strode, and his hounds chased clouds. Around midnight, a family of quail floundered into the air. Then nothing for an hour, except that the corpse of the goat, made high by a hot day, fluoresced a gentle green.

Then, from somewhere between dream and the forest, there was a breath. The grass by some rhododendrons moved against the wind. The feathered heads of the grass bowed towards the tree. Suddenly a tiger stood in the clearing. He never bothered to sniff, for his confidence and authority were supreme. The grandfather had expected to be disappointed — had expected it to be distinctive enough, but smaller and less commanding. He was transfixed by its size and its silence.

As it paced nearer to their tree, the wonder mounted. It had, he thought, the face of a god, severe and terrible. He lifted the gun; then lowered it. The tiger ignored the goat, and moved on round the tree. It stood on its back legs, put its huge front feet against the bark, and stretched. They heard the joints crack. Perhaps the grandfather breathed out too fast, for there was a stiffening in the air; the cracking stopped, the claws dug into the tree and the world was tense. Then the colour of honey, a smashing noise in the grandfather's head, which was the gun's report, and a breath of acid smoke. Then a thumping like a deep drum, which was the tiger's limbs flailing and fading; the last paroxysms. Also a choking, gurgling sound. An owl screamed, the tiger had died, and there was silence again.

For a long twenty minutes the two stayed up the tree. They could not see the corpse, which was behind the grass, but they saw a dark pool of blood expanding through the packed dry earth at the grass edge. They were frightened and proud. It is something to kill a god. Also, thought the grandfather, what if it's not really dead, but only wounded? They came down with the gun loaded, and the great-grandfather crept towards the grass with it raised to his shoulder.

A heavy shadow lay like a log at the grass edge. The grandfather's father, jumpily fired two rounds into the log. Earth spurted up, which showed that they had passed right through the body. Confident now, he kicked at the shadow. His shoe met nothing. They searched frantically through the grass, with no proper caution; a toad broke cover, but nothing else. They looked again at the bloodstain, and it was a pool of dark draining from a tree bough. They searched in the sand by the base of the tree, but there were no marks there from the great feet, and no claws had torn into the wood. Yet the grandfather and the great-grandfather had seen the grimace on the tiger's face, had seen that a corner tooth on the left side was missing, had seen a slanting scar on the nose. There was a new kind of fear and a new kind of silence. They ran home.

At least that is how it was told to me by the man who knew about maize.

Imrat, sad one night, told how he worked in a paper factory in Mumbai. He was happy there, for there were beautiful women and lots of money, and he liked to dive off the jetty, swim down, catch hold of an anchor on the seabed and look up and see the wave crests silver against the sun: 'They ran fast to the land, as if they feared drowning.'

He shared a bed-sit with two other workers at the factory. He despised one of them for wearing bell-bottomed trousers and the other for eating pistachio nuts loudly at night, and for being unable to spit the shells accurately into the bin. But they had coexisted, content enough, for eighteen months. An innocent eighteen months, no doubt, but painted red in the telling. Inflamed in his memory, their chaste bachelor outings became expeditions of delicious depravity. But Imrat's utopia was not to last. He had been summoned by his father, a devout Hindu, and there was a distressing conversation.

'Do you make paper?'

'Yes father, I do. All sorts of paper.'

'And what is it used for, this paper?'

'For books, father. Good books. Books of poetry and books about philosophy and religion and agriculture.'

'Not magazines, or newspapers, or idle women's tales?'

'Certainly not, father. Only serious and worthwhile books.'

'Then you will never work there again. You will pack up your belongings and return here. We will find you a place with your uncle's firm.'

And that's what happened. His father, said Imrat, wouldn't have minded if he had produced paper used for silly, trivial things. But to produce serious, scholarly books was to promote the delusion that there were immutable truths that could be set down in ink. Nothing true, he said, could possibly be bound up that way. It was different with ephemeral writing. That was good, for everyone knew that it couldn't last – that it would soon be swept away. It told the right parable about language. But he wouldn't have his son work as an agent of delusion, a slave to the vanity of scholarship. The father's horror deepened when he learned that trees had to be smashed up to make paper.

'What could anything on paper ever tell you that the tree which has been destroyed to make it could not? Nothing. Nothing at all.'

Imrat said that he didn't really mind leaving Mumbai, because the wife he had found in the hills was fatter than the woman he had been going with in Mumbai, and knew how to stuff peppers.

Up by the rock, in the evening, big furry bees like whirring mice with knitting-needle probosces, dipped into the flowers in the unbrowsed places. They were clumsy and uncoordinated in the cold, and banged against my legs as I stood staring out to the north. I stood there most evenings. Sometimes a boy from the village came too, with his puppy brother who scampered, jangled a milk-can, and looked at the map of the world in my diary.

The boy sang, and I sang back, and the puppy gambolled right up to the edge, where for a thousand feet there were only clouds and the tracks of crows, then always back to our feet, panting and looking up in two ever-so-slightly different directions at once. The boy was twelve and wanted to be an engineer. The puppy was five and wanted to be an engineer too.

The mist sent them down the hill to goat, roti and dal in their house on a slice of terraced mountain. And as I walked back to eggs, books and a growing conviction that I was missing the point, I passed a man who was loudly angry by the creeper-trees, who had a white streak on his head which arched up and down in the night.

'Don't worry,' the boy said. 'It is wine-drinker. Over limit.'

The drinker had a shed by the temple, and his shouts, muffled by the fog, marked the wet track up.

I heard what had driven the man to the bottle. The rock here is a kind of schist, so the ground is silver with mica. It shells out when you scuff over it, and spangles your boots. Jagjit's friend told the story.

'The wine-drinker is from Hyderabad. He came to the hills to sell vacuum cleaners for his firm. He came in a motorcar, but of course when he came to Tala he had to leave his car and walk.'

Jagjit shook his head at the friend. The friend said, 'Jagjit is a true patriot. He does not want Indians to be painted as simple people before a – excuse me – foreigner.'

Jagjit despaired. The friend continued, 'As the wine-drinker walked, of course his feet began to sparkle. He looked down and thought, "I'm turning into a god." So he marched into the temple and told the people that they needn't worry, for Krishna was here again. An old man sitting there said, "Ganesh, surely" (for the wine-drinker was carrying his demonstration kit, and a vacuum cleaner suction hose, very like an elephant's trunk, dangled out), and the people laughed so much that the wine-drinker went mad.'

'Now that,' said Jagjit,' 'is very sad and very funny.'

The days filled up happily enough. I learned to read the rain, and to know when to huddle in the shops though the sun still shone and the clouds were white – knowing that the sky would shake in a moment and dowse the world. I learned when the leeches would bite, which veins they preferred, and which rocks the scorpions liked. I learned how to pull the sting out of a live scorpion so as to leave it alive for a while, but harmless and enraged, which was good for frightening sisters and schoolmistresses. I learned that there was a soft and eager girl in Nainital who was reading classics, and much else besides, at Oxford. I found a cave in the hill with a stinking pool, where bats hung like dry leaves in brown rows.

They said in the village that there were white worms in the pond, thick as sausages and long as brush handles, and that the langurs ate them, sucking them like spaghetti, if they were ill, or to celebrate the birth of a young one. I threw a hook into the pool one afternoon and trawled up and down. There were no white worms, just gobs of bat guano, dead bats and a video of Cliff Richard songs. The langurs did use the cave, though. A villager said that canny langurs could catch handfuls of bats at a time if they stalked up slowly in the day, and that they'd snatch and crush and stuff their mouths in a single jerky movement. 'Like the smallest child on the train,' said he. 'With sweets. The loudest crunchings.'

I got to know this man. He knew English, and there was a picture of the Sistine Chapel, torn from a newspaper, on the wall of his house. He said, 'Italy – now Italy. Now there's a land. Not like England, with many soldiers; but with many grapes and many motorcycles.'

'You've been there?' I asked.

'Soon,' said he, faraway and misty. He shook his head to scatter the dream. 'It is a fat land. Now England, is that a fat land?'

'Oh yes,' I said. 'It is fat right deep down.'

'That is good.'

'No, it's not good.'

'How strange are you English.'

His uncle had gone to Milan to buy a motor scooter, and

had rented rooms from a Venetian printer whose parrot could say 'Jude the Obscure' in English and recite passages from the Kama Sutra in Italian.

'Really?' I asked.

'Yes,' he said. He drew breath and told of the rats in the canals, a pedlar who sold wooden puppets which could climb up ropes, the echoing tombs of the kings of Italy, and a waiter who owned the osteoarthritic left femur of St Paul, and the hair from Nero's last haircut. Then he considered, looked worried, and said he didn't like anywhere but India, and that he had to go to bed so as to be up for the market in the morning. He had apples to sell, and they had to be bagged up that night. He stood up, opened the door of his house, and bowed goodnight as I left into the dark.

That was where I was – the dark. Not the companionable, whispering dark of India. I wasn't in India at all. I was in the lonely onanistic dark of my own temple, looking admiringly around at the teetering propositions from which it was built.

~

## Chapter 4

# THE FOREST

'A student came to a Zen master, and said, "I am seeking the truth. What state of mind should I train myself to have, so as to find it?"

The master said, "There is no mind, so you cannot put it in any state. There is no truth, so you cannot train yourself for it."

"If there is no mind to train, and no truth to find, why do you have these monks gather before you everyday to study Zen and train themselves for this study?"

"I haven't an inch of room here," said the master, "so how could the monks possibly gather? I have no tongue, so how on earth could I call them together or teach them?"

"How can you lie like this?" asked the student, outraged.

"If I have no tongue to talk to others, how can I lie to you?" asked the master.

The student said sadly, "I cannot follow you. I cannot understand you."

"I cannot understand myself," said the master.'

There are four life stages in the Vedic ashram system. The first is *Brahmacharya*, the stage of dedication to the great quest — to realise Brahman in oneself. It is entered into by bright-eyed youths and entered or re-entered by repentant, cloudy-eyed dissipates. Its music is that of sometimes quiet, sometimes exultant consecration. Then there is *Grihastha* — the stage of settling down. Wives and mortgages are acquired, children are born, cars are polished, lawns are mowed, businesses grow, fortunes are made. Then, when the children fly the nest, the wives sag, and the machinations of the firm become unbearably grey, there is *Vanaprastha*. The Hindu goes into the forest, and begins to prise from his soul the deadly things that have stuck to it over the years of domesticity. He pays off his debtors, and tries to pay off the demons too. He has been dying since he was born, and now is the time to do something about it. The house is sold; the business is given to the sons. He takes with him into the forest only the sacred fire, the cultic implements and, optionally and unusually, his wife. He lives off wild food; his hair and nails go uncut; his capacity for delusion is gradually ground down by austerity and meditation. Eventually he may see clearly enough to go into the final stage — *sannyasa*. Then he will wander alone through India, begging. The ties with the old life and the old self will have been severed; he will be teetering on the edge of enlightenment, or living in it. He will know his place in the mind of Brahman, or at least where his place is not.

It is a stern system, now rarely followed. It has generated immense spiritual wealth. There is nothing in the system that cannot be described very well in the words of St Paul.

I thought that my adolescent contempt for the suburbs meant that I had transcended *Grihastha*, and so I took a bus, a train, another bus and a rickshaw to a hot wood. In my rucksack, since I didn't know the botany of India well enough to live safely off berries, I had lots of tinned fish, a bag of apples and a sack of porridge oats. I brought very little else of any sort with me. In particular I brought no spiritual resources of any kind, as the episode brutally showed.

Things happen in woods, whether you are prepared for them or not. To begin with, you think that you've found things. Wisdom, later, tells you that you've found nothing at all, but that you are in the process of being found. Finding, in fact, is the business of being found. And to do that (as I now notice happens in all the Arthurian legends that I love the most), it helps to be utterly lost.

My bit of wood was about a mile from the nearest road. The road was a rutted, dusty track along which trundled occasional bullock carts loaded with improbable bric-a-brac going from nowhere to nowhere. Walking into the fringes of the forest I nearly trod on a jet-black cobra which slid into a stream, looking fiercely back over its non-existent shoulders.

I'd thought of building the sort of leafy bivouac in which I'd spent many a summer night in England, but when I got to the place where I knew I should stay, I couldn't bear the thought of looking up at the sky through something I had made. I'd thought of finding the edge of a glade, but I found that I wanted desperately to burrow as deep as I could into the wood. If I could have squeezed myself inside a tree trunk I would have done. So I kept on walking until, at midday, there was more shadow than sun, and I threw my kit down by the bole of a tree that must have been fed on the same light that shone on the Moguls.

I sat and I listened. It seemed to me that I heard with my nose: the silence here smelt different to the silence of the clouds in which I'd been living. It didn't last for long. It was a response to my own clumsiness. The forest was holding its own breath so that it could listen to me properly and watch more steadily. Soon it began to breathe again. When it began, it did not begin tentatively, with a tweeting of little brown things. It exhaled suddenly and loudly. A coucal lumbered through the bushes by my side, booming to the sky. A brainfever bird began its own shrill frenzy, and a wave of noise crashed over me. Colour exploded out of the green. The fallen leaves undulated with the life burrowing under and over and through. A Bush Rat sat on a branch, looked at me, and beckoned with its nose to another.

Over the next few days I lay for many hours flat on the forest floor, my face in the mulch and my eyes at the level of a bandicoot. I saw the gently depressed roads through the leaves where the mice ran; the questing antennae of the woodlice; the aphids tapping columns of plant sugar; the delicate shifting shadows cast by little things. I looked into the ancient eye of a mildly modified dinosaur (a Green Barbet), which was trying to work me out. Because I was still for long enough, and because it does not live for long, in three days I became part of its memory as old as my memories of life as a ten-year-old. For the gnats and the fireflies, I was a part of the landscape, known for several generations. For all the animals there I am a folk memory. Each thing here lived its whole life with an intensity I could not match for a single heartbeat, and with an intimacy of relationship with everything else that has no parallel in any human experience other than marriage and parenthood. Each came from a family incomparably older than the crass hairless ape.

I saw ants taken by a Jungle Babbler, a babbler taken by a Shikra hawk, and a Shikra eaten by ants. I lay there watching the wheels of karma turning; wheels within wheels; intricately geared; powered by thirst, pain and desire. My wish to bury myself in a tree now seemed morbid – a wish for annihilation of something that I called myself. I ran from the wish and stood up, suddenly the tallest animal there. It was a journey of six feet and about three million years. The perspective, the intimacy and the fear dropped away. I brushed the last of them off with the last few leaves in my hair. I'd failed the first, ecological stage of the process of identification with Brahman. I slung my pack on my back and walked back to the road.

~

## Chapter 5

# FURTHER UP

*'I think what I really mean when I speak of the unconscious is the substance of the soul, the "centre" where all the faculties, sense, feeling, appetite, imagination, intellect, will, have their roots. Here all are merged in a deep, simple unity, open at once to God and to nature. Primitive man lives from this centre and that is why he is so "natural", with so much grace and spontaneity in body and soul, so open to God and to the infinite, and yet so readily turning astray into immorality. As the faculties develop, especially the intellect and will, man grows out of this centre; he becomes specialised, one part is repressed at the expense of another, he becomes "unnatural", complicated, disunited, yet develops a strong "moral" character to keep things in control. (This is typical of the British in India)...'*

— Bede Griffiths
*Letter, 1956*

~

'It's a good thing to see new things,' said Jagjit one wet evening.

'Yes,' I said, and carried on writing.

'Don't you think?' said he.

'Yes,' said I, 'I do.'

'Don't you think it's important?' he persisted.

'Yes,' I said, ' I do.'

'Don't you think it's dangerous not to?'

'Go on,' I said, putting the work away. 'Say it.'

So he began one of his set-pieces.

'Very well. A woman I knew, a friend of my mother, liked a predictable world to snuggle into. So she cocooned herself in all the usual cotton wool of domestic stagnancy. She never read newspapers, for they were different everyday. She preferred to see photographs of her children instead of the children themselves, for the children got bigger. Her son's moustache was distressing because he hadn't had it when he was small. Her house was deliberately cluttered, because, she said, if it were simply and sparsely furnished, she'd notice a small shift in a chair or a box or an ornament. Also the natural entropy of things meant that things would be disordered more usually than they'd be ordered, and to be usual was, she said, to be good. Also, she got rid of her little horse.'

'I get the picture,' I burst in. 'What lesson do you think I need to learn?'

Jagjit could be very didactic, and he thought I should be taught many things.

'Simply,' he said, 'that the great thing is to be vulnerable. She came to a sticky end, as you'd have discovered if you'd let me finish. The invulnerable life is the life not worth leading. To be immune to everything is to be fatally infected.'

Then he picked up his book again, and started to read hard.

Jagjit came to the leech pool one afternoon. I was standing in it, my trousers rolled to my knees and a good crop of leeches draining my ankles. He had been standing for a while by a patch of reeds, laughing gently.

'Mad Englishman,' he shouted. 'Come back to the land and be normal. There's some news.'

News was strange stuff, so I waded in, sat on the bank and bottled up the catch while Jagjit came round to me.

'A holy man's arrived.'

A sadhu who had studied at Varanasi, conjured ghosts in Lhasa and spent three days and three nights submerged to the neck in icy water in Sikkim, had come to stay at a monastery fifty miles to the north. There was to be a festival and a ceremony involving the spontaneous production of fire from a live sapling.

'He's a clever man,' Jagjit assured me. 'And at the least you'll be entertained.'

There would be dancing and, because it was some kind of fertility rite, a communal brandishing of a wooden phallus, carved from a tree sought out that year by the lightning that comes with the monsoon.

'You'll get lots of notes,' Jagjit said, encouragingly. 'And if you don't find it inspiring, you'll find it filthy in a whimsical oriental way.'

The trek would be a hard three days. There was no

metalled road. We would stay with the families of people who had painted Jagjit's eaves. We were to leave in three day's time. I said I would go.

'Good,' he said. 'We'll have fun.' He told me about the sadhu. 'He's very young. Barely out of his spots. And very direct. It is said that he attained enlightenment when he went into a betting shop in New Delhi to back a horse running in a dirt-track race in America. As he walked up to the counter, he took a slip from the dispensers on the walls. He turned it over and the back was coloured a deep blue. That, he knew immediately, was the colour of the void: the wallpaper of Nirvana. He felt himself falling into it, and awareness suddenly invaded him. He was, if you like, enlightened, transcendent, initiated. Actually, of course, the story is a lie.'

'Then how did it happen?'

'It didn't. He doesn't know enlightenment. He just knows, better than most, the vocabulary of enlightenment. Which makes him more useful to other seekers than a real Buddha. Besides, he'd say that a really enlightened man would never ever know that he was enlightened. You'll have guessed he's more Buddhist than Hindu; he's a great integrator. He treads along many paths, and draws whatever water he needs from whatever pools are along the way.'

'You say a great integrator; I'd say a cynical, confused opportunist.'

Jagjit clapped his hands in delight, and rocked backwards and forwards on his heels. 'And so would he,' he laughed. 'So would he. That is exactly what he'd call himself.'

I was annoyed. 'But what if, just if, that is in fact all he is? If someone acknowledges his own fault, and can describe it in more detail than an outside critic, it doesn't mean that the fault isn't there. Quite the opposite. And it makes acceptance of the fault more culpable, not less.'

'Fact?' asked Jagjit. 'Fault? Culpable? What a stilted Calvinist you are, though you shaved your head and stared at candles.'

'Thank you,' said I. 'And I never shaved my head.'

'Perhaps that was your big mistake. But though you are bigoted, presumptuous, and think only in straight lines, and even then feebly, I'd like you to come to Shalayi.'

And so I did.

Jagjit woke me early on the morning we were to go. Perhaps he had been in the room for a while, for I was dragged into the dark foggy dawn by the grate of a chair leg on the floor, and I prised open my eyes to see him sitting by the desk, his head cocked to one side, holding the monkey foot. Standing up, mock servile, he poured tea into a cup and handed it to me. 'Sahib, if you please, your porters await.'

Just the two of us went, of course. It was not a journey of ecstasy. We set off along a red road, woven in a hound's tooth pattern of tessellated brick. We sweated thinly and unsatisfactorily with the altitude. Water hung heavy in the air. It was like walking into a cold flannel. Half a mile on, Jagjit found that he had forgotten a box of chocolates, meant as a gift for the sadhu. He trotted back for them, and I watched a black fly, drugged with the cold, stagger into a wall. When Jagjit returned, he said that the sadhu would be very amused if we'd eaten lots of his chocolates by the time we arrived, and so it was our duty, as good guests, to do just that. So we did, until we both felt sick. Then we got up and went on through deepening fog.

A few traders paced the road, bracing loads of firewood, blankets or aluminium pots on bands round their foreheads. Jagjit saluted each one.

'A good morning, good father.'

'You look strong, mother.'

'Such hard work will make you quickly rich.'

They flashed bad teeth.

Probably the landscape was spectacular, but the mist seeped into our ears and clogged our tongues. We knew only the fall of our feet. The eave painters were good people, but we were tired, and I cannot write of it.

Shalayi, the village where the sadhu was staying, was a mean place of uncut stone and corrugated iron. The valley still climbed; the faces were still not flat, though the moods were. These were sharp-nosed plains Indians — old Aryans with stringy throats and rounded consonants. They were suspicious without being interested. They drank tea and rain water. They hadn't discovered the *chang* that makes dancing Falstaffs of Tibetans and Nepalis. Theologically they were on a lulling syncretistic cocktail. Hinduism trudged up from the plains with the bead traders, the sacred water sellers and the tinker musicians. The tantric Mahayana Buddhism of Tibet trickled down from the snows. Ecstatic animism grew native in the thin soil, giving eyes to the rocks.

Stale bodies and ammonia came at us. A yellow dog with a red sore on its forehead like a puja mark raised its head from a pile of rubbish and pattered over. Clusters of children in doorways clung to the lintels and jumped for a view of us, shrinking back as we passed. A plastic fire-engine lay smashed in a puddle; a door swinging in the wind had a creak with the pitch of voices, paced like speech by the breeze.

That night we were to sleep amongst the ropes and the milk powder in the general store, but first there was the sadhu to see.

'We won't talk this time,' said Jagjit, 'but there are respects to be paid.'

So off we went, up a twisted mud-river, leaving puzzled pi-dogs behind, to a stupa, stuck to the ledge at the foot of a glissade of fine scree. We knocked a dragon's tail on a wind-bleached door. The sound bounced off the rock and hit us twice. I'd thought there would be a mighty shuffling, a long wait and a great unlocking, and that something wizened would poke out and query. But the door opened smartly, and there was a brisk smile attached to a yellow robe. This was Dilip.

'This way,' said Dilip. 'Bob is playing cards.'

'Bob?' I hissed to Jagjit. 'Who's Bob?'

'Who do you think?' said Jagjit. 'The sadhu.'

'Bob?' I said. '*Bob*? He's supposed to be an Indian holy man.'

'He's all those things.'

'But – Bob?'

'Yes, his real name is Pandit. But he prefers Bob. He was in America. And also he says that the sound "Bob" is very like the name "Om".'

'Oh,' I said, 'oh,' feeling weak.

'And what game does god play? Whist? Gin Rummy?'

'All of them,' said Jagjit. 'You are not to doubt divine omniscience.'

'This,' I said, 'is sounding like a very poor script from a very cheap play.'

Dilip led us through a long corridor and pushed open a low door covered with green felt. The room inside was very dark. A spirit lamp jerked out bands of light. Blinking stupidly around, I saw a man sitting cross-legged on a rug near the lamp. 'Well,' he cried. 'Hi there. Isn't it Jagjit and his English friend?'

He put a fan of cards carefully down, and jumped up. He had a thin, pale voice. A Bronx accent was ladled over the quizzical Indian vowels. He rushed at Jagjit, hugging him close, and pushed him out at arm's length to see him, chattering excitedly in Hindi. Then Jagjit nodded his head towards me, and the sadhu looked. He was a plain-faced, button-nosed boy of perhaps twenty-two – brown, wild and elfin. There was a twist of his lip I didn't like. I thought he could be cruel. He raised laughing eyebrows at me and bent in a half bow, half nod.

'Well,' he said. 'Hello to you.'

'Hello,' I said, sullenly. 'Are you really called Bob?'

Jagjit smiled, but there was a sudden cold earnestness in the sadhu. 'Of course,' came the grave answer. 'Why not?'

We didn't stay long that night, and though Jagjit spoke always in English, the sadhu replied in Hindi, clipping his sentences short.

'He doesn't like you,' said Jagjit, jumping over a puddle on the way back to the store.

'I'm not devastated by that.'

'You don't like him?'

'He's hardly had a fair trial; but on the basis of an unfair trial, no.'

'You think he's too young?'

'Not at all. I think he's petulant.'

'Ah. You think he's too young. He said that you wish for mystery and at the same time disbelieve in the possibility of mystery, and so you are a cynical discontent with whom he can do nothing.'

'I wouldn't trust him to do anything with me. He's arrogant to presume that I would.'

'He said you'd say that.'

'And that, I suppose, makes him omniscient and prophetic?'

'It certainly suggests it.'

'You expect far too little of your gods.'

'And you expect too much. You expect a display of qualities that have no parallel in yourself. You expect gods to be made of different stuff, rather than just bigger.'

'Only in a way. I'm made in God's image, not he in mine.'

'Ah. A quote. Always the retreat into revealed truths. Never the confidence to assert anything yourself. Isn't it an insecure god who feels the need to indulge in occasional episodes of indecent historical self-exposure? Isn't it a god without the consistently forceful personality you'd hope for in a god?'

'Either that, I suppose,' I said wearily, 'or a god who realises he's displaying to people with defective eyesight, and talking to the deaf.'

'Anyway,' said Jagjit, 'Bob was annoyed at himself for not liking you. He will do better next time. He apologises — well, sort of — for talking in Hindi, but says it's nasty and dishonest to pretend he doesn't feel things.'

I was bored and wet. In thinking what to say to Jagjit I'd gone calf-deep into a pot-hole full of cold mud. When I reached the store, I squeezed my socks into a drain, got inside some rice sacks as well as the sleeping bag, and was asleep soon enough.

While the dark still clutched me, there was a clanging racket and Jagjit danced into the room looking stupid in a tunic and tights. The clanging was outside, but Jagjit wasn't. He pranced around for a while, and then beat me round the head with a bag of razors until I kicked his legs from under him, sending him backwards in a cascade of spam.

'I suppose this is your festival?' I grunted.

'Yes. It's good?'

'From what I've heard, no. From what I've seen, definitely not.'

And I put my head inside a sack. But the cacophony grew, and so did Jagjit's insistence, and there was no peace in the sack. I got up. Jagjit took my arm and pulled me to the windows. We'd missed the main procession, but still a crowd packed the street, and a platoon of highly burnished little girls banged on cans with bones.

We elbowed and waded through the throng. Where the road broadened to become the backwater where everything drained and remained, there was a frantic carnival. I'd thought that this was a village whose wretchedness was neither caused nor mitigated by alcohol, and I was wrong. Women were pouring potato-peeling spirit out of jerry cans into the tin and plastic mugs the merrymakers held out. Even the oldest faces winced, quivered and then smiled. The hordes settled around a central clear space, kept clear by a ring of sweating heavies who held bamboo poles between them and pushed the poles back against the bellies of the front-row spectators. Sawdust rose like snow with every stamp of the figures in the centre.

The figures were crowned with antlers – great proud antlers (which was strange, for only the little muntjac run wild in these hills). Their faces were stained a greasy blue-green; huge stiff phalluses were strapped to their loins. And, sure enough, just as Jagjit had said, they circled a tall wooden post, carved into the form of a penis, which was cradled by an old woman sitting on a canvas deck-chair in the middle of the dust cloud. The dancing had some pattern: the dancers stamped in rough sequence and the weavings were loudly choreographed by a young stag in red paint. But there was no obvious coordination with the clang of the cans beaten by the crowds. A beggar collected offerings of the potato spirit in a plastic Mickey Mouse cup. He staggered over to the phallus, poured some of the spirit over it and over the old woman's head, kissed the glans, and collapsed to loud applause.

'She,' said Jagjit, pointing to the old woman, 'is the oldest accredited virgin in the village. And these,' (he pointed to the dancers) 'are her sons.'

Jagjit wore little scholarly spectacles that day; they misted up as he laughed, and fell off as he doubled up to laugh the better.

'Well,' I said to the storekeeper, who had found his way to us. 'What is it about?'

'The mostest drink, and the food. It is very big, you see, and sweet like candy, but teeth not black, not fall out.'

Alternative versions, from other villagers, included:

'Very niceness, and the most smiles.'

'Much dancing, you see, over there, and the meat of many goats.'

'All day drink. All night drink. Then sleep, if not very, very sick.'

Jagjit was enjoying himself, spinning round in his jester's kit, dribbling with mirth. 'Oy,' he shouted, seeing me. 'Oy, Englishman. I look very stupid, eh?'

'Yes,' I said, and then the crowd swirled and swept me off to another corner of the arena, and I lost him for a while.

When I saw him again the sweat had cooled, and I was

cold and ready to go. The clattering had become a muttering chant, and the people were dispersing or sinking cross-legged to the ground, swigging and repeating the old invocations, crying out to old gods they were too drunk or too young to name. I'd been to affairs like this before and had expected the sadhu to be carried in at the climax of it all, on a papal litter and a surge of orgiastic fervour, to be welcomed as a new avatar.

'Oh no,' said Jagjit, 'he holds a quiet surgery at the monastery. We are due there now.' We retraced our steps of the previous evening. Others were going there too, but we'd missed the rush, and passed only the old and lame.

The sadhu was holding court to hundreds in the large stone room where he'd been before. The blue jeans had gone. He wore a long saffron robe with a row of red stars embroidered into the hem. He sat cross-legged on a gold cushion. Visitors' garlands of paper flowers were draped around his neck. He slumped forward. His hands were pressed into the hair of an old woman who knelt before him. His face was turned to the floor. I could see from the side that his eyes were screwed tightly shut, sending creases radiating over his cheeks to his ears. He was talking in a low mumble to the woman, and she turned her head a little to catch his words better. He stopped talking. He lifted his hands and lifted his head. He had the same face as the evening before, but there was a new tiredness and a desperate sorrow. The woman remained kneeling. An acolyte in a pale linen gown slipped out of the shadow, took the woman gently by the arm, raised her up, and led her out of the room. We were still at the door. She pushed past and bustled through a side door into the drizzle. She sobbed in great heaves. The sadhu smiled almost naughtily when he saw Jagjit, and bowed soberly when he saw me. He motioned to the acolyte. We were ushered forward through the throng until we stood before the sadhu. He remained seated, with his head bowed on his chest, and we sat too. There was silence in the room, unlike the cheerful hubbub I'd known before in such audiences. Outside, a prayer flag slapped the rosewood shutters.

Jagjit's face was set hard; his jaw twitched. His earnestness alarmed me. We sat like this for ten minutes or so, and shuffling began in the standing ranks behind. When the sadhu lifted his head, I started. Tears flooded his face; those flippant eyes were sad and deep and red. He stretched out a hand in benediction, making as if to touch my face. His fingers shook. Moved, I took the hand; it was cold and limp. He turned to Jagjit with a half smile which drained fast from him. 'It's a terrible thing, this sadhu business,' he said. 'Look at the people. They suffer so much, and trust so much, and I can do nothing except refuse to tell them their trust is unfounded.'

'The woman was helped,' said Jagjit.

'She thought she was, but I no longer think that that is the same thing as being helped.'

Jagjit was suddenly tired. He squeezed his eyes briefly shut and said 'We'll go now.'

'Yes,' said the sadhu, 'but come tonight.'

'We will,' said Jagjit, and bowed.

'Yes,' said I, and bowed too.

We saw the sadhu that evening, and with us came David, a dreadlocked American anthropologist we'd met at the festival.

The sadhu barely acknowledged Jagjit. There was a nod as we came into his low room. Then he turned to me: 'You are enjoying your trip?'

'It's very interesting.'

'You are enjoying your trip?'

'Sometimes.'

'Why are you here?'

'I don't really know why I'm in India, but I am in Shalayi because Jagjit asked me to come.'

'Why did he do that?'

'Ask him. Because he's my friend, I suppose, and because he knew I'd be interested.'

'*Interested*? And you are interested? In what?'

There was an awkward pause. I looked hard into him, and saw something I did not understand. Before I could answer he spoke again. 'You are English, yes?'

'I come from England, if that is what you mean.'

'You want to ask me some questions?'

Then again, before I could reply, he began again. 'Of course you do. What is it this time? How much of you will survive your terminal cancer? Are carnivores haunted by the ghosts of all the animals they've eaten? Or is fucking a good thing?'

'I'd like to know where your certainties come from.'

'That's easy. From Boston.'

He turned away to the American. 'And you? Where do you fit in?'

'I don't think I do.'

'Good answer. You're a Christian? I've met many.'

'I'd like to know what you thought of them,' said the American. 'I don't know what I am. If it helps you to call me Christian, that's fine. But it probably means more to say that I'm a Zen Buddhist with a Redeemer.'

There was a pause, and then a grunt. 'You studied Zen?'

'Yes.'

'Where?'

'In New York and LA. For several years.'

'So how can you be a Christian also? I don't understand. You must be a heretic to both creeds.'

'How interesting that you describe Zen as a creed,' replied the American. 'I agree with Zen's description of the human condition. The language in which the diagnosis is expressed is different from the Christian language for the same syndrome. But it's valid and sometimes helpful. But the therapy Zen proposes is hopeless. The Christians, I reckon, are right about the cure. Nothing else is radical enough.'

The sadhu curled that lip. 'I was wrong. You are no heretic. You've understood neither Zen nor the Christians.'

The American coloured. He asked the sadhu if he knew the tale of Avalokitasvara.

'Of course. But do tell me your perception of it.'

So he told the story of Avalokita, who attained Enlightenment. As Avalokita was about to enter Nirvana, he looked back and saw a rabbit with a broken leg. He was shattered at the sight of this suffering, and begged to be able to delay his entrance into Nirvana until he could stop the anguish of the world from which he had been liberated.

'The story is stranger and stronger than that,' the sadhu broke in. 'Avalokita vowed that he would never enter Nirvana until all other creatures could enter it with him.'

'Yes. And the request was granted, I think. Not only that, but he was given a thousand eyes to see the suffering of the world, and a thousand arms to do something about it.'

'That is the story, approximately. Why do you tell it?'

'Because Avalokita had everything to which the Zen student aspires. He saw with perfect clarity. He was at the end of the Zen road. And yet his insight convinced him that the fulfilment of Zen aspirations is utterly inadequate. Enlightenment is purely and simply enlightenment. It highlights the predicament, the diagnosis. Something or somebody has to intervene to address the basic problem faced by all created things. The things can't do it themselves – it has to be done for them. The world has to be condescended to. It has to be rescued.'

'Is this where I'm supposed to say: "Ah! There's suddenly light. That rescue operation has been done by the Christian God. How wonderful"?'

'That's right,' said the American.

'You're mad,' said he. And perhaps he was.

Mad or not, the American was stabbed to death for his wallet a fortnight later, and so got an early chance to test his hypothesis.

Jagjit was quiet as we walked back to the shop that evening. This was a quiet not of reflection but of exhaustion. There had been many colours spinning in our heads; mesmeric sleep came fast on the rice sacks.

I wanted to press on north. I'd heard of a great green glacier, green because moss grew on the ice. I wanted to see it. There was also supposed to be a crescent-shaped moraine of glacial rubbish where yeti bones had been found. This was a three day tramp from Shalayi. Jagjit was fed up with walking, and couldn't see the point. He said he'd wait for four days, and drink tea. The road was obvious enough, and I could manage without him. After four days he'd make his way back to Tala. He was expecting a book about Neolithic burial practices.

Before he left, he asked people about the yetis. Apparently they were everywhere. Everyone had seen them. A bit further up the valley you could hardly move for them. They had big feet and lots of hair. Some people's yetis walked on four legs; some on two. Mostly they were brown and shaggy, and disported themselves on snow and scree slopes. They were never found on the flat. Someone even said that there were clockwise yetis and anti-clockwise yetis. The clockwise one always travelled clockwise round hills, and their right legs were much shorter than their left to compensate for the steep gradient. If forced onto the flat, or forced to change direction, of course, these yetis were badly handicapped. If you wanted to catch a yeti, all you had to do was to chase it onto a flat area and throw a net over it or, even better, force a clockwise yeti to go anti-clockwise, or vice versa. If this was done, the yeti overbalanced and tumbled down the hill, falling stunned into the arms of the waiting hunters. This variation of a tired universal joke was a sad attempt to be funny. It was not part of my education in mythopoeia. It was simply fatuous, and myths are not.

Several homes in Shalayi had yeti scalps. They were made of goatskin and reverenced. One woman, Virama, had the penis of a young yeti. It was wrapped in a piece of blanket and kept in a biscuit tin. It had been severed, she insisted, after her late husband had stabbed the yeti to death after an epic crag-side struggle. It had been severed, her next-door neighbour said, from the decomposed body of a yeti which had stumbled over a cliff in dense fog. I bought Virama a cake and asked if I could see the penis. She went to the reliquary and unwrapped a long dried mushroom of a kind common in the plains.

Bob and his entourage were moving north too, tugging light from under bushels in some of the little villages I'd be passing through. I had no wish to join his cosmic circus, and planned to move out straight away to get a couple of days between us. He heard I was leaving, and he came into the shop as I was pulling the drawstrings on my bag tight. He was sorry if he had been offensive, he said, and told me to eat treacle each morning of the journey. 'For power,' he said. 'And strength and sweet breath.' He gave me a number in Minnesota to call if I were ever there, some letters to post (one to MasterCard), a small piece of liquorice and a koan.

The koan was a version of the famous Zhaozhou's dog koan. I turned it over and over, and it probably did part of its job.

*A monk asked Zhaozhou, 'Does a dog have Buddha-nature or not?'*
*Zhaozhou answered, 'No.'*
*Another time, a monk asked Zhaozhou, 'Does a dog have Buddha-nature or not?'*
*Zhaozhou answered, 'Yes.'*

Years later I was thumbing through a book on gazelles in a second-hand bookshop in Damascus. This koan, written on a piece of writing paper from the Baron Hotel in Aleppo, fell out. Someone had struck it through in red ink, with lots of exclamation marks and New Testament references. Zhaozhou would have loved that.

If you didn't know that the Himalaya leapt into the air when a continent collided with Asia and crumpled it upwards, you'd guess it after lying on it for a while. It has a grumbling unease, as if it's expecting further abuse. Earlier in the evening, a pylon had flared up in a huff of magnesium. The people were glad, for it was like a party. Then the electricity went off, but they were still glad. My eyes stung with smoke from the fire on which they'd undercooked the goat and overheated the curd. I had a homely kind of snuffle. I had a book to read and a head torch to read by. I wanted to drink tea until the roses flowered, and could think of no particular reason why I shouldn't. I looked out of the shack where I was sleeping, and saw the road winding steeply up. Sheer slopes are the sternest imperatives of all.

Grey dawns are slow things that never really happen. I walked out into one, and was glad it would watch me move. Shalayi was hard to shake off. I walked past the pans strung like bulbs, the airline T-shirts on hangars and the children begging for nothing in particular and finally, suddenly, the mountain was there. There was a huge green wall to my left and air to my right. The slanting light made greens yellow and yellows brown. The river water was smashed to spume. The road was grey schist and shingle; leeches looped over it and squeezed through the eyelets of my boots. My world dripped. To look at the blue and white prayer flags jostling in the wind was to know cold water poured from a height. There was rain on the legs of a girl from Harvard who was unaccountably there too. That night I shared a smoky shelf above a hut-fire with a grunting porter who was ferrying cooking-oil and who had leech bites on one foot in the shape of a swastika.

The next day, Emily, the Harvard girl, got up early, made porridge for us both, and went down to the river by herself. She sat on a rock for an hour in the lotus position, completely still, and brought the stillness back with her to the hut. It was not the sort of stillness that you interrogate, but the sort that interrogates you.

The path glowed. If silence could shout there would have been a deafening echo. Up above us, noiselessly high, brown water surged through a narrow rock throat. The small birds in the rhododendrons ignored us, and neither the rock nor the pines cared that we were there. I did not know to whom the prayer flags were praying. Emily was smiling gently at the mountain, but when she took off her boots I saw that blood had seeped into her socks. There was sun somewhere up there, but so far away that it didn't seem to matter. Eventually it went away, and then it did matter. We dropped down into the mist, and there were lights ahead. Emily drank whisky and sang about a seaman who'd two-timed his mistress and been killed for it. Moths filled the empty tea-glasses, and they gave us Molotov cocktails to light our bedtime books. The straw mattresses were damp with fog and kerosene.

'Good night,' said Emily.

In the morning she was gone. She had left in the dark, on her own, two hours before I got up.

There was no green glacier. There were no yeti bones. And I was glad. If they were there to be found, Emily would have found them.

Shalayi was damp and dull and familiar. Jagjit had got fed up and left, leaving a message on a piece of cardboard with the butcher: 'I am bored, see you soon.'

It was an easy, despondent trudge in the rain to Tala. The gardener was piling up oil drums on a patch of mud as I entered the compound. He nodded, and carried on stacking. It was temple time. The bells were muffled by sandalwood-scented fug. This was a killing day at the temple. A family walked up the track between the firs. The father swung a white chicken by the legs. The son clutched a pigeon, which flapped and fouled his dhoti. The Temple in Jerusalem must have smelt of blood and shit and fear.

In my room, everything was at right angles to everything else. Someone had put a carrot top in a saucer by my bed, and it had sprouted into a fluffy tree. The windowsill had been painted, the toilet used inaccurately, and a snake-skin had been nailed to the door against demons. A book on southern India I'd left behind was open on the desk at a photo of erotic temple carvings. My torch had been stolen.

Tala was suffocating me. I'd run out of adjectives; I was stupid enough to think that that meant that I'd understood, and could move on.

When I was due to go, they killed a goat for me, which was nice of them. I still don't know how much of the time had been wasted. I had some drawings, some leeches in small bottles of formalin, intermittent diarrhoea, and a wad of prejudices. I was glad to have had some job to do – something to fidget with – for otherwise the world would have whirred, and so would I; my mind would have spun and made me queasy. I would have manufactured little facile commonplaces to act as beacons, and would have come to regard those products of my own head as genuinely fixed points. This would have been dangerous. That is why I was glad to have leeches to think about.

I went by myself. Jagjit had to go to the Punjab. His father was having his varicose veins stripped, and the cheese still had to be carried from the churns to the post office. Anyway, I was starting to annoy him. He had been very demonstratively patient over the past fortnight. Friendship was hardening into hospitable duty. He thought I was a vacuous dilettante, collecting without classifying, observing without sympathising.

I was new enough in the country to feel nervous at the loss of someone I'd depended on, but he was irritating me too. He knew no difference between tolerance and uncritical acceptance, so he tended to regard belief in fallacy as a virtue. But he was a great talker and jokester, and confronted the world bravely. There was real pain when the bus wrenched us apart, leaving him standing in the drizzle. Shankar had given me a small sack stuffed with scented leaves to make me sleep, and a list of bespoke sycophancies to lavish on English scientists for him. I'd also acquired a packet of custard cream biscuits, a peacock feather, several family photographs (one in a broken tiger bone frame), a pot of herbal diarrhoea pills, some verses from the Koran on a piece of silk, a pebble licked by a toad (which sometimes cured warts), a copy of *The Spy Who Loved Me* with alternate pages missing, and a bottle of black potion, whose label proclaimed that, if taken at any time during the first six months of gestation it would cause 'sex reversal of the foetus'. A woman I'd seen mopping up blood had pushed this bottle into my hand, whispering, 'You must have beautiful sons. Give them to God.'

I slept on the bus, waking once as we plunged into a mat of cloud, again to see children chasing a dog which held a rat in its mouth, again as the other travellers piled off the bus to yawn and squat, and again as the driver went to offer honey to a roadside deity, put the sandalwood paste mark on his forehead, shave in a tin mug, and belch. And then I was asleep while the bus wove round hairpins with sickening drops and chugged down through the forest into the plain in a haze of oil vapour.

Delhi was as Delhi always is. It muttered and hummed as I shuddered through it in a rickshaw. A cloud of parakeets gusted over Barakhamba Road, and then the city was a mesh of light and shadow, hanging from flapping kites on invisible strings.

The birds make the only definite noise in Delhi; the rest is barter, chatter and hoof-fall, and the sound (which must amount to something) of thirty-five million eyelids snapping shut against the dust. Cardboard towers sprout from golden bulbs, and after nightfall the sun stays in the red walls. But it's the eyes of Delhi that you notice. They are more obvious than anything else and more obvious than anywhere else. Eyes set deep in faces, crouching behind noses, lurking in paan stalls, hiding in creases; all of them in shadow. It is mainly in the eyes that you see the other things that there are – the cows chewing, the fires flickering on the dumps, the flies, the battlements, the cool mosques and the strain.

At the station the whole world writhes, and nowhere is there a straight line unbroken by curve, glint or tone. The bad lights in their wire frames bend the place, deepen it, sprinkle it with metaphor. To sit down and read prosaically a prosaic book, you've got to brush away the litter of allusion that covers the seat. It makes poets and pretentious bores out of the most sensible people. At Ghaziabad, a very fat and very well organised Indian in immaculate white pyjamas got into my carriage, read and annotated the previous day's copy of the *Wall Street Journal*, followed it up with a mildly pornographic magazine, and went loudly to sleep lying flat on his back with his palms on his nipples.

Among the suitcases and the fighting children at Varanasi station lay a white-shrouded corpse on a wicker stretcher. The flies winged in and out through a cloth fold. In my room at the Gawdalia I put down my rucksack in my room away from the traditional route to the bathroom taken by the ants, and wandered out past the silk stalls, the masala houses and the paan shacks to the ghats.

Mother Ganga was fast, brown and broad, and had a film of holy oil and body fat. I jumped onto a boat steered by a pox-pitted wild man, and rowed by a little groaning boy whose back was crystalline with salt. We strained upstream. Orange garlands circled past; pilgrims ducked and gasped and swallowed and splashed. The boy levered us bumpily up towards the quiet crowds around the shrouds to where the orange of the flowers and the white of the shrouds becomes the orange of flame and the white of ash. The roofs of the riverside buildings were scalloped and almost Chinese. Monkeys paced on their knuckles through the temple courts; tangle-bearded sadhus with gridiron face marks in red grease sat slumped in doorways. The sweat was so thick on me that a mosquito would have drowned if it tried to bite. Thunder grumbled not far away.

In the night, rain roared inside my head, and there were the odd sharp punches of dream that the tropics often deal.

Blue-white tentacles arched over the river to lick monkeys from the temple tops; a livid red Ganga boiled and fumed.

In the grey morning cold, the ghats were sadder and death even more alien and hard to bear than it had been in the afternoon.

My room looked directly onto the heavily plated tower of the Golden Temple — a knobbled armadillo of a building with a bicycle shed on the roof. When the bells and cymbals of the night got too much, I went out to a café where a vulture-man, stooped from hunching too long on branches, gave me tea.

'That man,' another Indian said to me one night, pointing out the proprietor, 'has the largest collection of souvenir key rings in Uttar Pradesh. His uncle was killed when a lammergeyer dropped a goat's bone on his head.' Behind the café, from a house draped in festive lights, came a constant drone of chants in Sanskrit, the ancient Hindu sacred language, already old when Hebrew was first spoken.

'Do they all know what it means?' I asked an elderly professorial type who I'd seen in the café reading Chaucer.

'Do they know the words? Probably not. Do they know what it means? Possibly. Will they come to know what it means? Hopefully. Does it know what they mean? Without a doubt. And now, if you'll excuse me, I ought to get back to the Canterbury Road.'

In these temples there were giant orange elephants, coconut stalls and carvings that leapt and writhed. But the main feeling was *uterine*. It was dark and wet, it smelt of blood, and there was a deep thudding of maternal artery-drums. Not too far away there were screams. A candle wavered in a cow's breath, misty through a thousand years of stale incense. Hanuman's lips were full, and glistened with mango. This was a place of meeting and becoming.

There was really little point in me being in Varanasi. I would like to go there again now.

~

*Chapter 6*

# ON A HOT PLAIN

*'I, the fiery life of divine essence, am aflame beyond the
beauty of the meadows. I gleam in the waters, and I burn
in the sun, moon and stars....I awaken everything to life.'*
— Hildegard of Bingen

~

*'And if the wine you drink, the lip you press
End in the Nothing all things end in — Yes —
Then fancy while Thou art, Thou art but what
Thou shalt be — Nothing —
Thou shalt not be less.'*
— The Rubaiyat of Omar Khayyam,
Trans. Edward Fitzgerald

~

I went to Barakhamba, right on the Nepal border. It's in the
plains, but only just. Asia arches its back here. The Himalayas
hang over the place, and the mountain birds fight with the
dust sparrows for the seeds on heavy grass heads.

I woke with someone shaking my shoulder and shouting and pointing to the ground. My bags were pulled from the belly of the bus. I stood by them as the bus rattled off towards Kolkata.

I walked down the road to a chai house and sat down on an upturned fish box. The box was the property of the Governor-General of Queensland. A circle of children gathered. They asked for biros. I gave one to each of them from a bundle in my bag. They looked baffled and disappointed, but didn't ask for anything else. I drank a cup of tea, and then another one, and then Kamalesh arrived.

'Hello,' he said.

'Hello,' I replied.

'Good morning,' he said.

'Good morning,' I replied.

'It is very good,' he said.

'Yes,' said I. 'It is.'

'May I sit down?'

'Please.'

'My name is Kamalesh.'

'Hello, Kamalesh. I'm Charles.'

'Ah, Prince Charles (laughter). And Charlie Chaplin (more laughter).'

'Yes.'

At this unpromising point, a European-looking man with a long matted beard came up. He was dressed in a ripped T-shirt and baggy red pants. He sat down on a box between us, said, 'Howdy', in an Alabama accent, and rolled a cigarette with terrible concentration.

Kamalesh ignored him.

'Welcome,' Kamalesh said. And after more thought and a long pause, 'To India.'

I thanked him.

'You are resting here?'

'I hope so. For a time. I want to visit the ashram.'

I thought the American was probably from the ashram of Lonbutyai, two miles away up the hill, and said this loudly, hoping he'd take me there. He showed no sign of having heard. He had taken out an old copy of *Time* magazine and was drawing moustaches on the faces of the UN Security Council delegates.

'Not good,' Kamalesh shook his head.

'Why?'

'Much noise and much reproduction.'

I bought Kamalesh a cup of tea. He asked me what I'd been doing. I told him about the leeches.

'I have a cousin,' he said, 'who hates leeches. He makes canoes in Thanjavur. The water-leeches there are very stupid and they suck on the bottom of the canoes so that the boats are black and wriggly and don't move fast through the water. My cousin says that ten leeches are worth one mile per hour.'

I asked him, as I was clearly supposed to, what they did about it.

'At first, they painted the boats with paraffin, but that only worked for a month at a time, so now they pay boys to dive everyday into the water. The leeches stick to the boys. The boys come out and roll around in a pit of salt and the leeches fall off and die. Now there are very few leeches there, and the canoes can go fast.'

I supposed that all this was completely untrue, but Kamalesh was desperately anxious not to disappoint me. He was looking carefully and hopefully at me as he finished the story, waiting to see if it had pleased. So I smiled, and his face collapsed in a relieved grin. He drew breath, and started on another tale.

'A friend of mine once worked as a guide at Keoladeo (a big bird sanctuary at Bharatpur in Eastern Rajasthan). He knew a crane there. It was a famous crane because it had no eyes. It had lost first one eye, and then the other, when leeches had stuck to the eyes and sucked out all the juice.'

I must have looked doubtful, so he said, 'Cranes, as you no doubt know, cannot blink very hard. It's not unusual for a crane to be blinded by a leech in Keoladeo. But the unusual thing about this crane is that the leeches stayed. One end was embedded in the socket and the other end dangled out. It was strange to see. When the crane came onto the mud to sleep in the sun, the leeches pulled themselves into the socket and curled up inside so that they didn't dry out. But when the crane was fishing, you could see these little black fingers writhing round on each side of the crane's head. The crane had had the leeches for several years and seemed quite happy.'

'But cranes hunt by sight. How could it possibly fish with no eyes?'

'That is the strangest thing. I'm just coming to that. That is what my friend said to himself. He said, "How is it that

the crane can fish? It has no eyes. And it needs eyes to fish."'
There was a long pause. Kamalesh swallowed hard and began
again. 'Leeches have eyes. And leeches are very good at seeing
and smelling fish. So this crane would put his head gently
into the water. The leech on the left would look around for
fish on the left, and the leech on the right for fish on the
right. When one leech saw or smelt a fish, it would start
straining towards it. The crane would feel the pull and move
its head and its open beak in that direction. And so it would
catch the fish. Sometimes, of course, both leeches would
detect fish at the same time. At first this confused the crane.
It would move its head directly forward and miss its meal.
But after a few months it got to know that the right hand
leech was more reliable, and so it would move to the right if
there was any doubt.'

'Was it a thin crane?'

'Not at all. Very fat and happy. It had lots of eggs. And
the leeches were fat too. They had constant blood, and of
course they wanted the crane to catch lots of fish, so they
tried hard.'

I bought him another cup of tea and some balls of cream
cheese splashed with rose-water. He dipped them in his tea,
losing several. He asked me what it was like in London, if I'd
ever seen Buckingham Palace, and about the cost of potting
compost.

He had grown up in Pondicherry. His father had been a
waiter at a guest house in Auroville, the self-proclaimed
utopian town founded by 'the Mother', Sri Aurobindo's

Vice-Regent. Kamalesh's father had been sacked when, in 1977, the Pondicherry police had burst into the guest house waving their batons and brandishing the prejudices of most of the Pondicherry locals against the Aurovillian foreigners. The pretext for the search had been drugs. A large quantity of hashish and several hundred weights of carrots were seized. Three hens were trampled to death. Clearing up afterwards, Kamalesh's father had absent-mindedly hung a photograph of the Mother (there was a copy in every room) upside-down. When questioned by the Ruling Committee about the offence, he had said that it was difficult to know, in bad light, which way round her head should go. The Committee was outraged. Kamalesh's father stole a typewriter on his way out of the administration building and earned his living as a two finger typist from then on. 'She was a heavy-jowled woman,' said Kamalesh. 'I can understand his difficulty.'

Kamalesh came from a very religious Hindu family. He had calculated that a quarter of his father's tiny income was spent on flowers and dates for the household deity Kartikkaya, the war-god son of Shiva and Parvati. This taste for dates was an inconvenient one. Dates don't grow in that part of Tamil Nadu, and are expensive to buy. But there was no choice. Kamalesh's father once tried appeasing the god with bananas, but was bitten by a dog and lost a hundred rupee note. The god was plainly responsible because the letter K jammed on the typewriter. Double portions of dates for a fortnight were needed before Kartikkaya was propitiated and the teeth marks healed over. Kartikkaya was an unusual god to choose, and the family, said Kamalesh, regretted the choice. 'It would have been much easier with Ganesh. He's not so demanding. But my father started the devotion when he left the army. He saw himself as a great fighter, and so he reckoned that he and Kartikkaya saw eye to eye. And even now, despite the hardship, my father insists that the years of devotion are a good insurance policy. "Hanuman or Lakshmi in easy days, fine," he says, "but when there's real trouble, you'll see. You'll be glad we've backed the right horse. A proper spiritual Derby-winner."'

Kamalesh had five brothers and three sisters. The family apartment, in a stained tenement block, had two small rooms. One was divided in half with a curtain. Half was a living room, dining room and bedroom. The other half was a puja room where the image stood and where the offerings were made. Kamalesh's father recited verses from the Ramayana there every morning, dressed in a seamless robe. When he was going away from home to visit relatives he typed out the full text of the verses he would have chanted (using his own system of transcribing the Sanskrit into Roman letters; he didn't have a Sanskrit typewriter), and left the bundle of papers, wrapped up in brown paper and tied tightly with string, in the place before the image where he would have stood. He marked the position of the parcel on the floor with white chalk and put a cross of hairs across it so that he could tell if it had been moved. He always put into the bundle his grandfather's watch and the relevant texts for more days than he planned to be absent, in case he was delayed. The watch was to assure the god that Kamalesh's father knew that he should hurry back to resume devotions.

'Come to my home tonight,' said Kamalesh. His wife had got a box of special oranges from a friend in Goa, and there were some chickens to kill. I knew no one in the town, and agreed to go with him. As we rose to leave, the American tore a page from a diary, wrote a name on it, and gave it to me. 'This is who I am. You want to come to the ashram? Anytime. Ask in the shop.' I thanked him, and said that I'd come, but he was immovably back in his magazine.

There are no tenement blocks in Barakhamba. Clusters of breeze-block huts with corrugated tin roofs are scattered through the paddy-fields and the woodland fringes. It was one of these huts, next to a mound of shattered buckets introduced as 'The Fire Station', that was Kamalesh's home. 'Mon Reppo' was etched into a board nailed on the door. 'Continental influence,' Kamalesh said, pointing to it. As we ducked inside, there was a flurry, and a small alarmed woman in a sari stood rigidly to attention.

'My wife,' Kamalesh said. 'You may shake her hand.'

I did. She bowed her head and shuffled off fast into the next room, looking twice back over her shoulder. We sat down on mats. A hurricane lamp oozed yellow, undulating light. There were a few books – Hindi texts and some sensational English paperbacks – between bookends on a table in the very centre of the room. On the wall were some pictures – several highly coloured prints of Hindu mythological scenes; an advertising photo, torn from a magazine, of an Air India 747 taking off from Bombay Airport; and a page from an English scenic calendar, showing a thatched cottage in Oxfordshire engulfed by fuchsias. A large red-faced man in a leather jerkin leaned patiently on the garden gate.

'That house,' said Kamalesh, 'is called The Old Fire Engine House.'

I looked. It was. There was a sign on the gate, almost smothered with roses.

'Just like this,' said I, dutifully, and Kamalesh was very happy that I'd got the point.

Tea was brought. A chicken was strangled loudly in the backyard. Kamalesh took me into the puja room. 'It's not good that it's next to the kitchen. At least the last pujari said so. He said that the god might smell the cooking, and get upset with having only fruit. But what can I do? I cannot change the house. If I were rich I would get an electric fan to blow the smells away from the puja room. But I can only hope there's no trouble.'

Kamalesh had not taken up the worship of Kartikkaya. When he had set up his own home, he had budgeted carefully and decided that he could not afford it. He had adopted Ganesh, and had no complaints. He was concerned that his wife might have divided loyalties, though, and worried sometimes that he might be caught by the conflicting territorial jealousies of Ganesh and Santoshi Mata.

Santoshi Mata is a new Hindu goddess, created by the makers of a mythological film which was a huge box office success throughout India, but especially in Uttar Pradesh. She makes no appearance in the Ramayana, the Gita or the Puranas, and said some embarrassingly un-Vedic things on camera. But she was the perfect designer goddess for women throughout northern India. She appealed to domestic prudence. She was cheap to propitiate, and needed no elaborate rituals or professional priests. She was intensely practical. She did not insist that busy housewives stop scrubbing the potatoes and work instead on understanding that they and the potatoes were identical with Brahman. She responded quickly and sympathetically to requests for electric mixers, sons or television sets.

'My wife is a very independent-minded lady,' said Kamalesh with pride and regret. 'She goes to drink tea with other ladies from the village. They get to talking about religion. Then one of them will say, "Santoshi Mata gave me relief from my cystitis," or "the Compassionate One gave me low interest credit from the Mukherjees on the cooker," and my wife comes back saying, "We must have Santoshi." I say to her that she must not say these things, for Ganesh will be angry. And it's not that we've done badly. We have this place, and four children, and I was able to send my wife's father to be burned in a fine style at a very good ghat in Varanasi when he passed on.' Kamalesh took down an album from a shelf. 'It is forbidden to take photographs at the ghats, but here he is, at our hotel.'

The photograph showed a bamboo bier bearing a white shrouded body, lying on the coffee table. A single wreath of orange carnations rested on the shroud, and the family was smiling in the background. The television was on.

'By the time we got him to the river he was drowned in flowers. Which was just as well. It was July, and hot, and we had brought him on the slow train from Delhi. My wife had a watering can of lavender water, but still the journey seemed a long one. By the time we reached Varanasi he was quite a fat man, which had always been his wish in life. Eventually God is good.'

When they pushed the blazing raft out into the current that would take it towards the sea at the delta, a kite swept down and picked up a charred foot, taking it high above the roof tops and the rickety temples. Kamalesh's mother-in-law saw it through the tears, clapped her hands, and said, 'See, Bindha is walking to heaven.'

It was then, said Kamalesh, that he first began to question the validity of the distinction he had previously maintained between 'myth-truth and truth-truth'. His questioning was not the struggle of an Aquinas with the dark Olympian gods served up with his Aristotle, or of a Christian Tolkien wondering how the resurrection myth of Balder fitted with St Luke's dry forensic account of the third day. Kamalesh had concluded (though not in these words) that the world is packed with metaphors which might or might not be personally significant. To be safe, you should act as if they are. It was an Asian Pascal's Wager. If the metaphors in fact mean nothing, then nothing is lost except a bit of time and effort. In any event, the process of acting in response to the message is an act of self-abasement; it shows that you acknowledge your dependency on the fates, and is therefore a good thing.

In other words he was highly superstitious. He always put his right shoe on before his left, and polished his spectacles in an anticlockwise direction. If he trod on a cockroach he spat twice to the east. If a water buffalo nodded at him while treading the ground he wouldn't drink milk for a week. If he saw a group of more than five egrets he reckoned that his wife would be exceptionally fertile in her next month. And every new moon he put a bunch of laburnums in a jam jar on the mantelpiece. 'They suck in the light and give it out slowly until the next new moon. The moonlight in the room keeps bad things away.'

The image of Ganesh in the room next to the kitchen was an expensive one, made of wood by his brother-in-law, who made temple images for export to Sri Lanka, and gilded by a devout college friend. The shrine had doors, just like temple shrines. This meant a lot of ceremony. When the doors were opened at the start of the devotion, the presence of the god, which had been building up behind the doors, blew out in a sacred wind. Once Kamalesh had come in the morning to find that the doors had burst open of their own accord, so intense was the pressure from repressed divinity. Only educated people had shrine doors in their puja rooms. Kamalesh brushed round the image with a bunch of birch twigs, changed the flowers, cut up an apple and put it on a saucer before the god, and anointed himself between the eyebrows with a dab of sandalwood paste from a pot by the flowers. All this could be done without the chanting.

'But one must not be casual,' said Kamalesh. 'Some of the priests are terrible. I knew one who forgot his words in the middle of a puja for the conception of a child. He carried on for a while with the text of the funeral service, forgot that, and finished off with his mother's recipe for dal soup, in Sanskrit. Nobody noticed, except the puja man's apprentice, who was horrified. In fact, the couple conceived a lovely son. The apprentice (who was fired by the puja-man after an argument) told the story. The poor child of that conception suffered terribly. He was nick-named 'broth' at school, and 'green-and-wet'. Finally he could stand no more of it, so he went to be a fisherman in Chennai, and drowned in a storm. Which shows that the vengeance of the gods is real, and that you must be careful.'

Kamalesh became mournful. He ate his rice quickly and turned the wick of the hurricane lamp low. He showed me silently to a section of the room cut off by a curtain. There was a mat there, a glass that he filled with water from a stone bowl, and a vase with a single dandelion.

The dusk was thin and yellow like a jaundiced child. A dark mass of monsoon cloud crouched in the west. Along the avenue of trees behind the house was an orchestrated chaos of cicadas – a rolling surf of harsh sound crashing onto a beach of wet leaves, surging and swelling and dying and coming again. The noise was not far from being painful; it hummed and whirred deep inside my head, forcing out everything else.

In the night a fresh wind from the north muttered round the roof corners, lifted them up and slammed them down. Kamalesh, curled up in a sackcloth coat with a pointed hood, stammered sleepy curses.

Awake and up in the early morning dark, Kamalesh swept a path through the dirt from his bed to the village shrine ('the path to the holy *is* the holy,' he said. This was not the Jain practice of sparing small creatures from the tread of the devotee). At the shrine he did the standard ceremony. Only then did he begin the ritual in his own puja room.

'To be communal before being an individual is the first prerequisite of a life subsumed into the whole. One day I'll be able to sit at my own fireside and be part of the whole there. But that is a long way down the line. I'm not talking about *fellowship* with the carpenter or the mechanic or the ox-herder at the village shrine; I'm talking about *inclusion* in them. To be part of them is to connect with the heavens. Before the worlds began, the ox-herder was. But to be included in him doesn't make me one of his organs. We are not dependent on each other or on anything. The carpenter is an irrelevance, and so am I.' That's what he said, but not quite like that. I always had to prod him into philosophising. Usually a frown at my speculations was the nearest he got.

His wife mixed the sandalwood paste for his anointing.

'Sometimes I say to her, "Today, my dear, red is the colour of joy", and sometimes, "Orange, I think, but not too bright, or the sun will be jealous of the blaze on my forehead". I taught her to say the mystical words as she mixes. That way the words are caught in paste, and the anointing has great power.'

Not many predatory vanities could withstand the flickering of a great sandalwood flame of colour on a saint's forehead, laced with the Gita. Kamalesh's father (a seer in his old age) once saw the vanities bolt. They were angry bundles of sparks spurting from the temples, banished by a chant, and seeking an unguarded home.

The bathing required by the rituals was difficult in a hot country. 'But all the more necessary because it is hot. The religious are cleaner and have fewer diseases. This shows that Hinduism makes sense, and is true,' said Kamalesh, in a rare appeal to the absolute. 'It is true, though, that in the winter Brahmins catch more colds.'

He had a low regard for Christians. 'What do they *do*? How can they break free from the wheel? Their religion does not demand enough of them for it to be credible.' He had had two encounters with Christianity, which together had immunised him solidly against it. The first was when a Roman Catholic zealot had handed him, as he came out of the temple, the memoirs of the French saint, Therese of Lisieux. He still had the booklet, and he showed me the passage that so outraged him. He had underlined it in blue biro, and peppered it with exclamation marks.

In 1896, Therese got the first signs of the illness that was to kill her. She was delighted. She wrote: 'At midnight I returned to our cell. Scarcely was my head laid on the pillow when I felt a hot stream rise to my lips. I thought I was going to die, and my heart nearly broke with joy. But as I'd already put out my lamp, I mortified my curiosity until the morning and slept in peace. At five o'clock, when it was time to get up, I remembered that I had some good news to learn; and, going to the window, I found, as I had expected, my handkerchief soaked with blood.'

'Pure, simple, life-denying perversion,' snorted Kamalesh. 'If that's sainthood, then I want to be a demon. Even that bird,' he swung his arm at a swallow diving past, 'has a higher view of life than that; more basic gratitude.'

The second encounter was with a Protestant missionary. 'God *crushed* his son for you,' the missionary had bellowed. 'I wanted nothing to do with such a god,' said Kamalesh. 'If omnipotence chooses child-killing, I'd rather have someone more limited but more kind. I'd never feel safe.'

Islam was better. 'I had a Muslim friend who sold his house in Lucknow to pay for the plane tickets to Mecca. There was some left over, so he dug up his father, reburied him in a Shiite cemetery in Iraq and paid a local man to keep the stone clean and mourn him each year on the anniversary of his death. My friend was poor from then on, and his wife was miserable, but they *deserved* salvation, and I'm sure they will be honoured.'

Kamalesh did not understand why Hindus in some parts of India made such a fuss about the Sikhs. 'True, their texts and their gurus pervert Hinduism. But if Hinduism's ideas begin to turn on a word or a phrase or a coincidence, then you have Hinduism no more, but rather a Western university course on Hinduism. How can you pervert someone who has seen all and been all and is all and comprehends all? You can't pervert Hinduism either.'

'Do you believe in God?'

'A more important question is: 'Does He believe in me?'

And so on, through the morning. When the heat got up, so did my stomach cramps. Lying on a mat near the kitchen, bathing in the stink of dal didn't help, so I got up and walked down the road to take my mind off it. I wanted to go to the ashram, but was unsure what reception I'd get. The place had a reputation for wild sensualism and a dogmatic lack of dogmatism. Kamalesh had said that the founding guru had died of botulism after eating a tin of pineapple chunks. The death was apparently commemorated and celebrated by a strange and blasphemous ritual called the ceremony of the Can of Bad Karma. Each year on the anniversary of the death, the members of the community who were qualified to instruct in meditation and yogic practice ate an enormous meal made solely from canned food. Acolytes chanted the scriptures as they served, and incense wafted their devotions heavenwards. Importantly, only the true initiates ate. The ceremony was supposed to show that theirs was a robust enlightenment, invulnerable to the corruption symbolised by tinned curried chickpeas. And also that they had overcome not only the fact of death but also the fear of it. To wield a tin-opener with untrembling hand was to show that the wielder had looked death in the face and that death, intimidated, had turned away its eye. It was playing canned chicken with eternity.

The original guru seemed to have some kind of redeemer function. The devotees felt that the founder had tasted death for them – that they were immune to it because of his spiritual lymphocytes. There were also, and less interestingly, the usual tales of sexual exploitation and drug-crazed parties; of wan pregnant Californian teenagers with flowers in their hair and needles in their veins; of tearful menopausal women used as foot-stools; and of pariah dogs with ribbons tied on their tails.

It seemed an innocent place that afternoon. The main gate was at the end of a tree-lined avenue off the highway. A cluster of cycle-rickshaw men snored at the checkpoint, their arms and legs all tangled like a ball of worms in a compost heap. An attendant in a long dhoti was asleep on a chair inside a sentry box, a truncheon dangling from a loop around his wrist. Waking resentfully, he asked what I wanted. I told him the American's name, and asked where the shop was. He waved towards a low yellow building across the compound, and fell asleep.

There was nobody in the shop, and only milk powder and picture postcards for sale. A curling calendar showed men in boiler suits and red helmets smiling out from an Esso refinery in Nigeria. Beneath it, an alcove in the wall, like a Muslim *mihrab*, held a plaster image of Ganesh. Incense dust frosted the floor. Deformed fans and rabbits frolicked across one wall. The door behind the counter opened onto a fenced yard. A hen was anting itself on a children's slide. From somewhere near, Western pop music pumped from a fading radio.

I walked into the yard and shouted. Not even the flies moved. Back in the main compound an Indian in a loin cloth was pushing a wheelbarrow full of chewing gum. I showed him the piece of paper with the American's name.

'Where is he?'

'Dead. Dead. It is a very great pity. He was a very good man. Come, I'll show you where we buried him. I dug the grave myself, and it was lined with grass and leaves from his home in Austria.'

Surprised that a member of an ostensibly Hindu community had been buried and not burned, surprised that an American should feel such attachment to Austria, and surprised that the young and apparently healthy man I'd spoken to three days before had died, I thought the grave-digger must be wrong. He was, but was only convinced of it when the American walked across and said, 'So you came. Greetings. Please come with me.'

He set off towards a nissen-hut. I followed, and ducked into the darkness after him. We were in his room. There was a low wooden bed against the far wall. The sheets were crumpled into a ball, as if torn off the bed and hurled back at it in vengeance for a disturbed night. He motioned to me to sit on the bed.

'Drink?'

'Don't mind if I do.'

'Whisky okay? We get it from the airport, so it's not bootleggers' crap.'

'Thanks.'

'This stuff is from LA. The wife brought it on her last trip. She comes to see me as if I'm in a zoo. She likes to see me pace my cage, and she always looks to see if I've enough litter in my tray. Obsessed with bowels, my wife is. Defecation is her only interest outside bead-making, sexual intercourse with my old friends from the office, and watching people give away money and toasters on the TV.'

It was a prepared speech, like so many I'd heard. And like so many people in India, he was watching for my smile. When it came, he went on: 'And so out of the ten days I see her each year, nine are spent in moans about Indian plumbing and hygiene, and in rhapsodies about lomotil. She doesn't fear boredom or malaria or damnation or meaninglessness, but she is terrified of amoebic dysentery. She carries with her, alongside her lipsticks and tampax, a little laminated chart with pictures and descriptions of stools in their various stages between a Californian maternity ward and a Kolkata mortuary. She got hepatitis once, went the colour of custard, and spent a week throwing up into a plastic bucket. But as long as her bowel movements were normal, she was a model of stoicism.'

He paused again, and gargled with the whisky.

'Why have you come?'

'I'm from England, and I'm in India studying leeches.'

'And so you come to us? That's very funny.'

He really seemed to think so, and he laughed a lot. When he stopped, he told me that he was called Mike, that he been at the ashram for eight years; that I could ask him damn well anything I wanted, and stay if I wanted to; and that he didn't believe for a moment that I'd come all the way from England to look for leeches.

He said that the ashram got a lot of journalistic prowlers at its gates, hoping for a publishable tale of vice. The orthodox Hindu papers were the worst. They wanted stories about the corruption of Hinduism, so that there could be passionate clarion calls to purity in the editorials and a flood of correspondence to fill the pages. These papers also tended to be nationalistic, or at least xenophobic, and no readers were lost when foreigners were pilloried. When copy was short the reporters would merely invent a story. The ashram would complain, and sometimes somebody was sent from the editor's office to investigate. He'd go into the village by the ashram and take soundings. The villagers would long ago have read the story in the paper, and it had become true to them. They'd swear to the investigator that they knew it was true; they had been told it by Rajiv next door. The investigator would always find that there had been, at the very least, a solid sub-stratum of persistent rumour to ground the original story, and he'd report back to his office that there was no need to publish any kind of retraction. And what's more, if a reporter were to go and talk to Mrs Akhtar in the yoghurt stall near the post office, she might be able to tell him something interesting. And so on. So the ashram had stopped complaining, and now watched the stories become myths with an existence independent of the facts that were supposed to have spawned them, and a potency far greater.

The sceptics in the village who had studied chemistry at college and realised that corroboration of facts was important, may have disbelieved the original rumours and scoffed at the credulousness of their neighbours and the poor referencing of the article. But they would never have disbelieved the myth which grew up. This wasn't because the chemists were really credulous too. It wasn't because of the awesome ability of mere repetition to by-pass all critical filters. It wasn't to do with the power of sentiment, or any instinctive connection with the folklore culture. It was to do with the independent life that the myth had acquired. Myths aren't parasitic. They don't need human hosts for their perpetuation.

Mike was convinced of this for an interesting reason. It was that he, who knew the fallacy of the original newspaper stories about the ashram, nevertheless believed the myths without question. 'And if I, uninfected by the virus of Indian subjectivism, cannot (not *will* not) deny the truth of the myths, then surely the myths must exist independently of their observers, let alone of their retailers.'

'I don't at all understand what you mean when you say that myth is true,' I said.

'I mean that it's changed its hearers, rather than being changed by them. Something's true if it creates or transforms, and untrue if it shifts with time or circumstance. If there's a conflict, as most of the great religions agree there is, between Truth and Untruth, Light and Darkness, and so on, and you define what's true as that which is immutable, it follows that the mutable is untruth, and to be repudiated by religious men. It also follows, of course, that something that changes other things must itself be unchangeable, and must therefore be of the Truth, and therefore true.'

This seemed nonsense to me. Plain lies, I said, had immense power to change people. There were plenty of ugly examples in the history books.

He didn't agree. If the 'lies' did change people, they weren't lies at all, he said. There must have been some error of perception or comprehension on the part of the people who labelled them lies. Facts were only worthy of the label 'facts' if and insofar as they proved their credentials by demonstrating their power to change people and events. All the world's religions agreed about this. Judaism and Christianity, for instance, asserted that God, the Truth, was first and foremost a creator. He created from nothing, and the world evolved. His hallmark, and therefore the hallmark of truth, was alteration of the status quo: in other words He changed things.

I said that he hadn't distinguished between creation and change, or, most importantly, between change for the better and change for the worse. The devil changes a lot of things, I said, but changes by corrupting. To worship *movement* in itself was silly. There wasn't anything good about going in the wrong direction. The mere fact of movement didn't tell you anything at all about the destination. His test ('does it produce the sensation of movement in the world I can see: alternatively in myself?') was grotesquely subjective. And what was subjective in metaphysics was selfish in ethics. He, as a Hindu, ought to know that selfishness was both a symptom and a cause of Self, from which he was supposed to be breaking free.

I said too that this was a strange and embarrassing first conversation to be having with a stranger, and he replied that it was a good talk to have, but that we'd gone as far as we could go along that road until I learned to regard paradox not as an impasse but as a bridge.

We went out together into the compound. He hadn't decided that I wasn't a reporter, but said that he'd show me round as a gesture of trust.

The centre of the ashram was the square formed by the low lying buildings that I'd first walked into. Some of these buildings were residential; most were assembly and teaching rooms. The ashram owned a satellite village of prefabs quarter of a mile away, across a belt of scanty woodland, and most of the community lived there. There was a steady core population of about a hundred, and at any one time there were thirty or so drifters as well, often ex-members of the full community who returned to wonder whether they should join again. They were put up in the ordinary members' accommodation and treated the same. There were a few families, and so a few children. The ashram ran a little nursery.

There were only a few Indians amongst the community. They were in administrative posts, but since work had to be performed according to a number of complex procedural formulae (involving specifically Hindu acts of consecration) they were full members. Almost everyone there was from

America or Western Europe. The Fourth of July had been mysticised and was celebrated by the chanting of specially composed texts which drew explicit and passionate parallels between the wrenching free of the States from Britain and the wrenching free of the enlightened soul from the bonds of Karma. At the head of the ashram was Sri Daloo, or 'the Father'. He was not there at the moment, and had not been for the past eight months. He was in Long Island, setting up a meditation centre. 'We're all excited by the Long Island project,' said Mike. 'Many more people will hear as a result of it.'

'Hear what?'

'Whatever there is to hear.'

Most of the community was at a lecture now, Mike said. He wanted to go himself. Would I like to come too? Of course, I said, what was the subject?

'Evolution. And the speaker is a very distinguished academic from Kolhapur.'

The lecture was in a high-ceilinged barn on the edge of the woodland. A large and noisy audience of westerners was already there by the time we arrived. They were all sitting on the floor; most had cushions, and many bowed at us. A jug of water was passed along the rows; people sipped and passed it on. An eight-year-old poured it over his sister's head and was told, 'Stop being dysfunctional.' His mother went out for a cloth and curtsied to me as she brushed past. The lecturer, a bulbous, sweating, smirking theologian, was ushered to a podium. He coughed and began, with a lisping sententiousness, and lots of italics: 'Brothers *and* sisters. Wherever I go within the Hindu world, I find grave distrust of what, with a tone of awe it does not deserve, is called "*modern science*". Of course, all the Mumbai Brahmins have refrigerators, but they apologise to *themselves* and to their observers about it, and are secretly happy when the power cuts out. It is Darwin's theory of evolution, though, that causes most disquiet in Hindu houses. It is the *shameful*, yes, *shameful, apotheosis* of the *Western* obsession with linear progression; the *antithesis* of the cyclical *Hindu* way of looking at the world. It is this *fear* that has robbed the Hindu world of *Hindu biologists*. There are plenty of *biologists* who are *Hindus*, and plenty of *Hindus* who are *biologists*. But that is *not* the same. My plea tonight is *this*: there *can* be and there *must* be *Hindu* (pause) *biologists*.'

(Applause and looks of mystification.)

There was lots of loud eating. The children, bored, were moving from pinching and hair pulling to punching and biting. A very beautiful Swedish girl, on a much sought-after seat on a vaulting horse, sucked on a piece of sugarcane, plaited threads into a friend's hair, and crushed lice between expensively manicured nails. Mike saw me looking at her.

'So lovely,' he said, 'but far too available and very flatulent.'

'*Perhaps* there is no conflict,' the theologian was saying.

'Consider a straight *line*.'

We all considered a straight line, except the girl and the children.

'A straight line is *nothing* but a *circle* of *infinite radius*.

Obviously, as the radius *increases*, the circumference gets *flatter* and flatter. We know that the earth is *round*, but it does not look like that to *us* because, when we look at the horizon, we see only a *very* small part of a *very* large whole. If we could look at the world from *outside*, without the limitation which our *size* and our *senses* put on the view, we would see the *roundness* of the thing *clearly*.'

Mike was looking at the Swedish girl, and seemed to see things clearly.

'It's the same with the *absurd* claims of the evolutionists. They think that the world is marching in a *straight* line through time, changing *incrementally* as it does. If they are *romantic humanist* evolutionists, they believe that the world is getting *better* all the time, is progressing steadily towards a *brave new world* populated by fully refined *super-beings*. If they are *deist* evolutionists, they are a bit confused about whether things are getting better (because they have a problem with the presence of evil: the grit in the clockwork), but are sure that things are progressing to some *great historical climax*. They therefore think it is particularly important *where* in time events happen. Indeed they are particularly keen on *events*. It is this that makes the Christians, for instance, emphasise the *historicity* of the Incarnation and the *events* of Christ's life. A Hindu, presented with the set of facts which constitute the raw data of the Christian claims, would *not* get so excited about them. For the Christian the significance lies to a great degree in the allegation that the events occurred in *historical time*, the same time through which *you* and *I* live. They therefore say that we can be *affected* by those events, and indeed could not be affected *except* by events occurring in conventional space and time. But the Hindu would state simply that the fact that the events were *available* to human senses and apparently occurred in the time through which we all *move*, would itself *necessarily* be an indication that they were *illusory*, the stuff of *maya*, and therefore *useless*. It is *precisely* that plane (on which Christianity asserts so loudly that it exists) that Hindus spend all their religious lives trying to *leave*.'

A Common Myna swooped through an open window, strutted up and down behind the speaker, and then stopped, its head cocked to one side, and looked at him. We looked at the speaker, and then back at the bird. The speaker took a small Disneyland hand towel from his briefcase, wiped his head with it, and went on. And on.

'A *Hindu biologist*, looking at the world, would say: "There seems, doesn't there, to be a *fairly* general rule that *real* things are *circular*. That is the *usual* form of *basic* things." Look at *atoms*. Look at *sub-atomic particles*. If *circularity* is the general rule, the burden of disproving the circularity of time, and of proving that the world is proceeding along a linear plane from *chaos* to *order* or from *lower* to *higher*, should rest on the *shoulders* of the Western linearists. The linear scientists are divided even amongst themselves. They assert the doctrine of *entropy*, the doctrine that *everything* in the perceived physical world has a tendency towards *disorder*, and yet they don't see that this *cuts* at the *root* of their philosophy of progress; of *directional* change.'

He stopped and drank some water. The myna left. Mike whispered, 'You see? He's good, isn't he? He doesn't mess around. He takes the bull firmly by the horns. It's reassuring to find the degeneracy of Western thought exposed by the exercise of Western wisdom. We're so often accused of taking cowardly refuge in mysticism. But there's no need.'

I said that the bull was getting much the better of the fight, and that the professor would be well advised to retreat into his mysticism and double-bolt the door. Mike looked at me down his long, sunburned nose, honking with pity.

Enlivened by a sycophantic clap and a wad of gum from the wheelbarrow, the professor started up again. I watched the girl. She was listening to the lecture now, and smiling, and rocking from side to side. A butterfly hung near her hair in a shaft of sunlight, and its tongue seemed to be licking the motes of dust that danced in the light. A child reached up a hand and crushed it. The professor was pausing between paragraphs, and I heard its body break. I could make no sense of this. It was pointless to think about the death of butterflies. It didn't get you anywhere.

Somehow the lecture ended. There was loud applause. The girl swayed away. I went with Mike into the yard. 'Come and see the ashram,' he said.

Most of the occupants lived in little low chalets. Most were single, many cohabited, and there were only very occasional marriages. The chalets were simple. Many were decorated with large posters of sunsets, mountain scenes, motorbikes and topless rock chicks.

'We don't discourage adoration of these material things, although the stricter gurus would think we were heretics. Most of these people will go back to the plastic world of canned music and the internal combustion engine. We'd be doing them no favours by pretending that they can live life there at the bullock-cart pace. We have to help them to build bridges between the sublime and the ridiculous, and to know that there's no real difference between them. They have to learn about the divinity in a Coke can. We're after robust spirituality.'

'How far are you along the road?'

'That is like a trick question from a Zen master, and I'll answer it that way. If I have or had a sensation of movement, it's the senses speaking and the Ego priding itself on progress. I disregard their voices. If I have a sense of my own static position, that position is, necessarily, defined only with regard to other points in the world. I can say nothing about their validity or even their existence, and so I know nothing about my own. The only intelligent people are confused people. In Hinduism we've mapped, named and systemised that confusion, but the confusion is no less for all that. Indeed, the Hindu genius is that confusion's own nature has been refined and developed by the process of description.'

For all his articulate talk of Hinduism, Mike's philosophy (although it hardly struck me at the time), was far more Buddhist than Hindu. I've never met a less contented or grounded Buddhist.

We were in the hospital. There were ten beds, none of them occupied. This was unusual. The ashram's occupants were said to be very fragile, and generally there was a case of hepatitis, dysentery or bronchitis.

The German medical orderly had a leech-myth for me.

A young woman had come to the ashram in the dry season. She was Australian who'd been travelling on her own in the south and had had doses of most of the diseases around. She had drunk from a very low and very murky waterhole in Kerala, and three weeks later had felt a tickling in the back of her throat. She coughed up some fresh blood and began to feel tired. By the time she arrived at the ashram she had difficulty breathing and was profoundly anaemic. The young Indian nurse in the daily surgery had looked in her mouth, gone white and gone missing. She didn't come back to work, but told her mother in the village that she had seen, down the Australian's throat, the snakes writhing on the head of Shiva, and that this was a terrible omen. She confessed to stealing a bandage and drinking the surgical spirit, resigned her post at the hospital and went to Chandrapore to marry, by way of penance, an old cycle-rickshaw man who had long been petitioning her father.

A doctor was called. He looked and gasped. For hanging on the Australian's uvula was a cluster of small leeches, attached by their rear suckers to the mucous membrane, their heads rearing unhappily in the bright surgical light. Getting them out was tricky. The hospital sent off to Kolkata for some ENT cocaine spray. Meanwhile things got worse.

The Australian was denied water in the hope that the leeches, dehydrated, would crawl out over her tongue if a saucer of water was held in front of her mouth. This failed. Then one leech went wandering and crawled into the nasopharynx. Its head, disgustingly, could sometimes be seen waving around in one nostril. Someone told the Australian what was going on and she vomited at the thought. The acid in the vomit detached a couple of the leeches, but the rest clung on. At last the spray came. The leeches were anaesthetised and plucked off with forceps, and there was an end of them, and the start of the myth.

That evening Mike talked about the organisation of the ashram. He was clearly regarded as a reliable spokesman. There were other people in the room, but they sat in the shadows, nodding quietly at what he said, and never correcting or adding.

'Many badly hurt people come here.' (Nodding)

'So our first duty, when a new member arrives, is not to discipline him or teach him our language, but to comfort him. Later he will learn that the relaxation possible when one is welcomed and the burdens lifted is a very high form of discipline, higher probably than anything he has experienced before. But we don't start with this lesson.' (Nodding.)

My hackles rose. 'You make them, in other words, wholly dependent on the community, both emotionally and physically? So that their defences are down and you can later trample where you want? So that they'll later take anything offered, however bad it is?'

Mike was not as outraged as I expected him to be. He looked disappointed. 'Compassion, even amongst the Christians, is generally thought to be a virtue.'

I asked if he agreed that compassion was directed, sometimes ruthlessly, towards the real good of its object, not its comfort, and he said that yes, it was compassion that chopped off gangrenous legs, but also compassion that anaesthetised the patient before the amputation. I should not conclude from that, though, that the members of the community were only nice to outsiders and to others for the purpose of lulling their objections to sleep: of stunning the capacity to criticise. I should conclude simply that the community thought that it was better to be nice than nasty, and that people could really help each other. He was not talking, he said, about love-bombing or manipulation.

After a little while (usually a few weeks), the new entrant would be invited to go to one-to-one meditation classes. He still wore his own clothes and hair. He'd be assigned to a teacher, who would discuss his progress with him and report to the principal – the guru. The initiate would be taught some simple Sanskrit chants, some breathing exercises, the least gymnastic yogic positions and some recreational meditation: thought-journeys and the trick of believing in the reality of what the deliberately confused senses were saying. The community did not encourage pupils to try these techniques alone: there had been some unfortunate experiences.

A Rumanian engineer had been following a series of

meditative adventures, described in a commonly available textbook of Buddhist practice, which involved imagining himself to be a particle of dirt in a great river. The book told him to feel the other particles all around him; to be wafted into the gills of a carp and out again into the white race of the upper reaches; to be gulped into the red dark belly of a sturgeon and assimilated into its muscle, helping to propel the fish downstream; to pass into the sun when the sturgeon was netted, clubbed and dried; to pass into the gut of an old woman who bought the dried steaks in a market, out into the earth when the woman died and decomposed, then to be washed back to the river when the big rains came, and out into the sea, before being spirited up to the clouds by evaporation and a high pressure system and dropped again at the water-shed where the river had been born. It was all harmless and classic stuff.

The ashram had been alarmed and embarrassed when the engineer's body was washed up twenty miles downstream from the mud bank from which he had been used to swimming. He was naked. His hands and feet were tied roughly together with nylon string. The police recovered his diary from under his pillow at the ashram. The last entry, in large capital letters, read, 'I bind so that I may be free: I know that by this paradox I will gain release.' The ashram was relieved to find, at the inquest, that the engineer had a long history of schizophrenia.

But there was no such comfort in Martha's case. Everybody loved Martha. She was Australian, and obviously sane and relaxed. She was also very pretty, but in a homespun way that kept the men from lust and the women from envy. She baked cakes, changed the babies and played the cello in the orchestra. She had played hockey for her university and tennis for the Queensland second team. She helped out in the ashram office, could type seventy words a minute and had a huge repertoire of card tricks and dirty jokes. She was slightly disparaging of the high spiritual ambitions of some at the ashram, saying that her purpose for being there was 'to keep clear of the freaks and weirdos you find in Australian clearing banks.' But her zeal was really deeper than this.

One summer afternoon, her teacher had taken the whole class on a thought-wander from Varanasi to Chennai and back again, via Kabul. This was elementary, first-grade fun. They'd even stopped off for a thought-picnic by a baobab tree, and had had metaphorical hard-boiled eggs. Martha thought it was a great laugh. That evening she told her room-mate that she was going to see a very nice man with a beard who had winked at her in Kabul. She giggled and turned off the light. In the morning some farm-workers found her body at the foot of a cliff near the ashram. She had jumped from the top.

'But these things,' said Mike, 'no more prove that our methods are faulty than the existence of lung cancer disproves the Christian premise that there's a loving God.'

If the new entrant's progress was satisfactory, and he was still enthusiastic, he'd be invited to enter the next stage. This was more demanding. It involved signing over to the ashram the title to any real estate held by the initiate. The transfer was not legally binding, and in fact the initiate himself could, and often did, hold the transfer document in his own personal strong-box. The purpose was to teach the entrant what material renunciation would feel like: to begin to loosen the ties that bound him to his home and his possessions. The entrants appreciated this gradual approach, said Mike; it laid to rest their fears about financial exploitation, and made asceticism seem accessible and reasonable.

At the same time, the spiritual exercises became more arduous. Meditation sessions were longer. At the end of this period, initiates could sit in the lotus position for twelve hours at a time, turning a mantra over in their minds and hoping that the mantra would eventually turn over their minds. There was more overt talk of the disposal of Self, or its identification with the mind of Brahman. Sex and alcohol were banned. The delights of the early meditative games began to seem dangerous, precisely because they delighted the *mind* and fed the merely rational presumptions of the acquisitive old life. The initiate was invited to shave his head as a sign that the old vanities meant less. Many did shave. Many did not, thinking that to be bald in a community of bald people was just a new form of the conformism they'd come to India to repudiate. This view, said Mike, was respected.

Most stayed in this intermediate stage for about eighteen months. There were no formal requirements for progression to the next and final stage; none of the confrontational vivas of some of the Zen sects, where a Zen master will ask the disciple a question which, to be answered satisfactorily, must be answered in a way which would be impossible if the question had passed through any of the mind's labyrinths. 'We are not Buddhists, and we have no tests of utter unreason,' said Mike. 'We're Hindus, remember. Many have travelled the Buddhist way, and talk in those terms, and it's fine if they want to look at things that way, but we see utter unreason as very advanced spirituality, close to enlightenment. That's too much to expect. If anyone wants to embrace chastity, meditate for twelve hours and sign over their wealth to charity, we presume that there's nothing much wrong with them. The principal can veto any candidate, but he never has.'

The next signing over of goods was binding. The 'charity' is the ashram. 'We support the poor in this area, and need to publicise the principal's teaching. We have a mission in Long Island, and are hoping to open one in Sydney.'

The life of a fully initiated disciple is demanding. It's life in a fairly (and the ashram would say benevolently) totalitarian regime. Heads are shaved. They don't tolerate any excuses about this being harmful conformism. The disciples are expected to proselytise, and success in proselytism is taken as an index of spiritual progress.

'If a man has properly dissected his Self away from his soul, he will be able to hold it fully out to the passer-by in the street. The sight of such a thing is immensely attractive; new disciples will be gagging for it. Everyone knows that holiness is magnetic. We know that holiness consists in this total alienation of self.'

The time spent in meditation is dramatically decreased. 'Why spend time practising meditation when you can *be* meditation? In this way we weld thought and action in a way which you'll no doubt write is antithetical to Eastern religion.'

Mike continued, with well-scripted fluency. 'Two things will surprise you about the full initiates: their normality and their happiness. You expect to see either dangerous fanatics or chronic, self-obsessed melancholics. Here there are neither. When you see that they are normal you'll have learned a great lesson. You'll have learned that the baseline state of man (you'd probably say the unfallen state) is to live without the Self. To seek primordial happiness you have to go into the primordial places. You have to get back to Eden, before the apple of self was plucked. When you see that they are normal you'll have learned that to abandon Self is to lose nothing, and gain the whole wide world.'

I was offended. This was transparently part of a convert-the-Christians brochure. I'd thought we were in serious dialogue. Actually I thought that this was uncontroversial stuff. I had only one quarrel with it, and it was not theological: I found the full initiates to be neither normal nor happy. Normal people are not at all happy, of course, but the unhappiness of the initiates was not a normal sort of unhappiness. If Mike meant that many of them were not as odd or as unhappy as they might have been, the rest of his argument was good.

Next day, Mike introduced me to Julian, a Canadian full initiate. He'd been a plumber. This was easy to guess. His spiritual language was full of talk about connections. He mixed his metaphors as an expert barman mixed cocktails. There was not always the same benefit from the complementarity of opposites that you get in a decent cocktail bar.

'You have to understand,' he said, 'that the only real insight is the insight that everything is connected, is a part of one organic unity. What you'd call heresy borders indivisibly on orthodoxy. The same tubes service them. And who is to say which is the more distant province? If you have no capital, who is the metropolitan and who the provincial?'

He was hectoringly non-dogmatic. 'You believe that two plus two equals four? Then you are narrow minded and stupid. You've not been told about all the alternative number systems. You are the poorer for it. You can have no conception of the multitude of alternative universes that are constructed according to these systems.'

Julian's six-year-old daughter had caught him in the matrimonial bed with the girl who did his business accounts. More baffled than resentful, the daughter had told her mother. Julian's wife, silently, and with no apparent ill-will, had hired a small van, packed her belongings, shot the dog, and gone to live with her mother.

Julian had gone to the airport, posted a set of instructions to his solicitor from the departure lounge, and caught the first flight to India. There was an article about the ashram in the in-flight magazine. He'd got on the bus to the ashram from Mumbai bus station, and had begged Mike for a meal and a place to sleep. That was eight years ago. Since then, Julian said, he had come close to complete victory over his ego. He had seen stars; he had dreamed dreams; he dismissed as commonplace the 'pedestrian spiritual strolls' of St Teresa of Avila and St Francis.

'Stigmata,' he said, 'are two a penny in Hinduism. In six months I could teach you to bore holes in your hands with your mind. It would just take a bit of fasting, a lot of meditation and a lot of morbid concentration on your palms. Your so-called subconscious, given a proper channel through which to flow, is a powerful thing. It certainly has no trouble drilling through bone and muscle and tendon. All you'd do is to bind a bit of body tightly to your psyche until they become entangled. Then you'd think of a plughole, and, hey presto, you're a fully authenticated mediaeval saint.' No, he hadn't actually seen such stigmata, 'but that is because Hindus, by and large, have more interesting and worthwhile things to do. Why should people want to pierce themselves? It's mere vandalism. The only worthwhile wrecking is the wrecking of the Self; and that's necessary so that reality can build on the empty site.' Was he confident that he could do the demolition himself? Of course he was. 'We have infinite strength.' He choked on his digestive biscuit.

Sue, who slapped him on the back, disagreed. She described herself as 'on the Tantric edges of Hinduism', and laughed, saying that she sometimes wondered if she was not really 'on the frantic edges of egoism'.

I had to get out of this. They let me sleep the night in the hospital. I woke before dawn with mouse shit in my hair, and crept churlishly down to the road, leaving an embarrassed letter for Mike, explaining that I thought he was a great chap, but that the ashram wasn't really my sort of thing.

I felt worse about abandoning Kamalesh. We had an appointment with a goat curry, and I knew that he wouldn't believe my honest explanation for taking off. But I needed air, a view, and some blue and white sky, and I triumphed over my conscience. That night I was in a crumbling hill station, happily watching some people watch me.

A doctor had taken me up. I'd been stumbling through the rain, anxious to get well clear of the ashram and its love-scouts. He had swerved to the kerb, jumped out and handed me his card. The University of Calcutta, it said. MB, ChB, and a Diploma in Sexual Health Medicine from London. 'In London,' he tittered, 'my sexual health was very good, believe me.'

He was perhaps thirty-five, stank of duty-free aftershave, and was a terrible snob, like so many educated post-imperialists. I was tired of meaningful conversation. I wanted to look out of the window and let the world slip by. But there was no escape from ideas. His every paragraph was a seminar, studded with axioms. They were bad seminars. I disliked them and disagreed with them. But out of habit I sat in the chai house that night and dutifully and distastefully transcribed them.

He had started as soon as my rucksack was slung in the back. The card did all the necessary courtesies.

'My people, they are dirty and stupid. They will not help themselves. They have been subjects too long. They cannot move except at the word of a foreigner. So I, an Indian, must become a foreigner to move them.'

I was clearly expected to respond. But he was one of those men who turns tongues to wood. I've known many, but very few have been Indian.

'That's sad for you?' I asked obediently.

'To be alien in this land? No. For my country is not India, but the medical libraries of the world. India is the kingdom of the dispossessed. To be a citizen I'd have to be a static refugee, to sleep with a little dirty woman, to have ignorance as my creed and indolence as my friend.'

He was fat. He took his hands off the wheel to wipe them on the trousers of his suit. A stethoscope trailed ostentatiously out of his pocket.

'Don't you blame the British? If India is passive, wasn't it the Raj which broke its back and left it dependent on command?'

'My friend.' He smiled confidentially and leaned closer. There was whisky with the aftershave. 'The British are sailors. They know the rules of the open sea. The sea laps at the shores of every land. So the British are true internationalists, seised' (yes, he really did use the word) 'of the rules which are the lowest common denominators of human action. Now the Indians – they are a big people, but a local, landlocked people with a long, pointless coastline. Their laws are the laws of the village. They have buffalo-minds – looking down, chewing steadily, fit for the yoke. This passivity is nothing to do with exploitation; it's a degenerative disease. It's what happens when you're stagnant for millennia – a deep spiritual prostration.'

It's not easy to know how to deal with this sort of stuff. So I said, lamely, 'You can't think the British were right to rule as they did? No one else does.'

'Why not? If the British had not ruled, someone else would have, and less kindly. The Indians have no imagination. That is another way of saying what I've already said. And unimaginative people, when they don't plod, can be brutal. The buffalo can trample horribly, and keep on chewing. The little rajdoms of old India were nasty things.'

The car lurched round a corner. Larch woods cascaded towards a bus, burned black, upside down in white water.

'True nationality,' he went on, 'is a function of fellowship. And fellowship has nothing to do with accidents of geography. I was born in Poona. I am a Brahmin. So what? To be Indian is to share in a fellowship of squalor. You live in the bookstacks, and so you are my brother.'

I didn't like this. I asked him where he was going. It triggered another lecture. He manipulated me into asking for it.

'I'm off to see an old woman. She is dying even faster than I am. Her lungs bubble and echo. They're hollowed out by TB, and fluid is rising into the holes it leaves behind. I could give her drugs to drain off the fluid and morphine to make her high. But these things are expensive. I doubt she can pay for them. So instead I'll tell her some lies, which come cheaper.'

'Does that worry you?' I regretted the question before it was out.

'Of course not. I'm helping, but helping at an affordable price — at an Indian price. I suppose you think this woman is precious; is made in the image of God. That's your brand of blasphemy, and you can keep it. But I'm a Hindu doctor. To me she is interesting. She, too, is made in the images of my gods. When she was young, she was like a Parvati, dancing along with Shiva. When she was pregnant and smiling, like Vishnu. Now she is like some other god. It's easier for us, you see, to know the divinity in things. But we don't think that divinity is boringly constant. We know that it is sometimes ugly and malevolent, and we needn't invoke your sophistries to sustain the myth of one ever-loving Being. We have no problem in walking round a children's cancer ward and then going to the temple. A Christian who goes happily to the ward and then to his church is insensitive, schizoid, or bloody ignorant.'

He spoke with the bitter second-hand fluency of the over-read and the under-recognised.

'The youth of Christianity is just one of the things that makes it ridiculous. Hinduism was already ancient when your cult was born; it can address fundamentals so well because it sprang up at a time when there were nothing but fundamentals around. The Jesus-sect is the new kid on the block — a fad that will soon fade or degenerate into fanaticism.'

He wound down the window, and lit a cigarette. 'Forgive me for saying all this. As an eight-year-old I was buggered by one of your priests.'

The smoke spouted out of his nose and billowed into his eyes. He began to talk wistfully about his time in England. He had a bed-sit off the Earls Court Road, and at first was very frightened of the tube train he had to catch to the hospital.

'I was a simple boy, remember. I thought it was a dragon. First there was a spitting in the dark. Then a grumble and a roar. And then, out of the earth, a silver snake. Other people weren't worried, though. They read their newspapers, and I admired them for their calmness. But then I began to think that I was the only one who knew it was a dragon. That was the first time I believed I'd got one up on an Englishman.'

The second time was when he'd prised a nurse from her English boyfriend. The doctor had lived with her in Earls Court for months, and loved her dearly. But she had run off, saying he was too possessive; that he was not ambitious for her; that he wanted a simpering slipper-warmer.

'I knew then,' he said, 'that I must learn the art of contempt. Jane had left me because I respected her and wanted to see her freed from the need to work. Wanted to see her calm and unhurried, because I thought she could use the calm well. To keep her I'd have to abuse and despise her. Western women want to be diminished. This, I saw, was a general principle. Despise in order to keep. Have contempt in order to command respect. That principle was England's great gift. Contempt is the most important British export.'

He talked on about sexual adventures, Windsor Castle, fish and chips, and the problem of Kashmir. Then on to a recent capital trial in Karachi, back to the idea of a State and on again to rent review in West London. He dropped me at a crossroads, and asked me to visit his family. 'There will be special tea. You have my card.'

'I have. Thank you. I'll try to come.' This was a lie.

And that was it. He drove fast round the corner and off into the rain. I didn't see him again. He was drunk and very lonely.

In the night a white owlet bobbed and peered at a silent lightning storm over the far distant Himalaya. The high tops flashed blue and yellow, the men in the chai house played cards, and one coughed blood and tried to pretend it was paan.

In the morning I hitched a lift in a Land Rover to a place where I'd heard you could buy myna stew. On the way we hit a cyclist. He swerved in front of us, was swept up onto the roof, and burst on the road behind. His belly was torn open, and the flies loved it. There was blood and dust in his hair, and his family rubbed their eyes and moaned in time with his spasms.

I went back to the plains and stayed there, looking for something I could not name, but which sang distantly and high, and which I have now been following all my life. I wrote down many things, but only one story, because I was young enough to think that propositions mattered more than stories. Even the story I wrote down signified nothing, and made me look rather good. I wrote about a wild incomprehensible argument that had blown up one evening between my landlord and his cook, a manic-eyed Dravidian with matt-black hair dribbling onto his shoulders.

The hostilities opened with a metallic crash, I wrote. Then excited scraping noises, a thud of wood and china, and a torrent of abuse, first from one, then from another, in a violent symbiotic duet, each drawing strength and passion from the other. The arias ran into each other until the music was lost. Then sudden silence. But only for a moment. For a busy, mounting, gibbering began. It went on like this for an hour, with sometimes a peal of clear scream. I lay on my bed, trying to read, and laughed and laughed and laughed.

In the morning, the landlord, Vishwa, slouched puffily into the kitchen where I was sitting, and dumped an omelette in front of me. It was nauseating: all oil and crisp. He saw me swallow unhappily at the sight, drew up a chair, and breathed over me.

'The cook, he is filth.'

'It's all right.'

'No, you are ever so very polite. But he smells, and eats cows.'

'Are you not friends?'

'With him? With that?' he spat. He indicated the omelette with disgust, as if it was the sullied soul of the cook, dissected out and publicly shamed.

'But why, Vishwa? You said that he worked hard, and had a beautiful sister.' Vishwa had rhapsodised to me, starry eyed, about the photograph of a slight, sunny girl by the Dravidian's bed in the old cellar.

'Beautiful? She is cheap and thin, And he, he—' Words failed. The cook was unspeakable. Vishwa tugged at my sleeve, pulled me through a bead curtain into an out-house, and pointed at a mound of willow-patterned rubble. It was the tea-set that Vishwa's mother had been given in 1947 by the English family whose blackbuck heads and colonial militaria she had half-heartedly dusted until the family, along with the heads and the campaign medals, climbed sullen and scared onto a Southampton-bound boat.

'I'm sorry, Vishwa, I'll buy you some more.'

'No, no,' he sighed.

'I'd like to.'

'You are a kind man.'

He chewed his nails and rubbed chip fat into his moustache. He was sullen. Then a new spark.

'I will burn his bed. His bed and his pyjamas.'

'You mustn't do that,' I said, with an unconvincing and unconvinced sternness. 'Pyjamas must be inviolate.'

Vishwa was leaving the room, a frightening purposefulness in his step. I'd hoped that pyjama-burning was figurative; that it meant that the cook would get no rest until he had atoned. But there was nothing figurative about the paraffin sloshing in the can that Vishwa now brandished. Nor about the fire in his eyes or the matches he had plucked from the stove as he opened the door to the cellar.

'No, Vishwa, no,' I said, managing to squeeze between Vishwa and the stairway which led to the cook's little damp bedroom. 'It is bad to burn people.'

'He is not a person,' said Vishwa, a new and alarming quietness in his voice. 'He is a pig, a strangler of cows, an unwashed good-for-nothing who never cleans his teeth.' The old passion was returning. The murderous, resolute pallor of his face was replaced with creeping redness. It was time for cunning.

'Really?' I said. 'Uncleaned teeth are disgusting.' I decided to risk all in a grand and dangerous venture. 'An aunt of mine only brushed once a week. She smelt, and we hated her. You are quite right to be angry. Burning is the least he can expect.' I stood aside. The stairs to the bed were clear. But Vishwa did not rush down. At first he looked at me with a new companionship. Then with surprise and puzzlement. And when he spoke, it was with the patronising reasonableness of the evangelist. He had regained the moral high ground. I was a savage. It was his duty to teach me the principles of civilised behaviour. His arm came paternally round my shoulders. He turned me away from the cellar.

'There is a better way, as our beloved Mahatma taught us.' He touched his forehead as a Catholic would cross himself. 'We, who know better than that sad fool, must be patient with him. He is primitive. We have had more turns of the wheel than him.' He was speaking to me, not to himself. There was no element of self-reproach. I was the pupil, he the teacher.

I saw Vishwa again that evening. He and the cook were drunk. They were playing very approximate draughts, chewing paan and spitting happily into a bucket.

When I put down my pen after writing this I thought that it was nicely observed, illuminating and shrewd.

I don't know what I would have written about all this now, or whether I would have written at all. The boy who travelled through north India collecting leeches, oozing confidence and dispensing certainty had intended to go to the south. Fortunately he got a massive dose of giardia and couldn't. It would have been a shame to have smeared the sacred south with his presumption and presumptions. I dislike that boy intensely. I have been trying to kill him ever since.

~

*Chapter 7*

# A SMALL HILL IN THE SOUTH

*'Bodhidharma sat facing a wall for nine years, meditating.
A Confucian monk came to him, wanting to be taught.
Bodhidharma sat still and silent for seven days and nights
while the monk pleaded for his attention. Finally the monk
could stand it no more. To show his sincerity, he hacked off
his arm with a sword, and presented it to Bodhidharma.*

*"Here is a token of my sincerity," said the monk. "For many
years I have been seeking peace for my soul, and I know that
you can show me how to find it."*

*Bodhidharma finally spoke. "Do not bring me your arm,"
he said. "Bring me your soul, so I can give it peace."*

*"But that's the problem," said the monk, "I cannot get my
soul, or even find it, let alone bring it to you."*

*"You see," said Bodhidharma, "I have given you peace of
soul."'*

~

The boy got fat, bald and bumptious, and went back to India.
Sometimes it seemed to him that he had learned something,

but this was not positive learning; he had simply shed some of his illusions and unlearned some of his errors. It mattered to him surprisingly little that he had not acquired any new knowledge.

On the south-east coast of India the crabs are big because the tsunami gave them the bodies of lots of fishermen. The people they ate were almost all on the edge of destitution. If the Hindu doctrine of karma is right, and our status and welfare in this life is a reflection of our behaviour in past lives, the average Indian must have been massively more evil than the average Swede. Karma subcontracts a lot of its work to the polio and rabies viruses in this part of the world.

Poverty is out of fashion in modern India; it is no longer romantic, as it was in the days of Gandhi and for several decades afterwards. Then the poor *were* India. They enjoyed a strange elite status. Now they are firmly outside again, on the dumps at the edge of the cities.

Going out of Chennai, we wove between the shacks that had sprung up on the site of the wave-wrecked villages. I got out to take some obscenely voyeuristic photos. A woman dropped an octopus onto the car and ripped open her toddler's shirt so that the lips of a fly-blown wound could beg more loudly for rupees. She wore a wooden cross. I gave her nothing, because I was ashamed. The child probably died.

Rising above south Chennai is St Thomas' Mount. The unhelpfully divisive legend says that this was where St Thomas was speared to death by a Brahmin, jealous of his evangelistic success. If he died here, his last view might well have been of the distant sea, fringed with palms and shuddering in the heat. There were no throbbing auto-rickshaws then, and he would have heard the surf crashing into the sand, and the Black-Headed Orioles fluting on the tangled slopes. But St Thomas' Mount is rather too symbolically perfect to be genuine. Thomas is yet another of the vicarious Christs that Christians inexplicably multiply. His death is seen to be redemptive, and so to follow his Master's pattern – on a hill, outside a city. Even his side is pierced by a spear, producing a wound like the one that convinced him of the reality of the risen Jesus. In modern devotion, the parallels are embarrassingly explicit. Up the steep path to the top of the Mount – the route that would have been taken by Thomas on his way to his death – there are the stations of the cross.

The happiest nuns I've ever seen frolicked and giggled and ate ice cream under a banyan tree, merrily pointing out the city landmarks, curtseying coquettishly to me and using their rosaries like conkers. Many people sat and looked at a cross that sweated blood during Mass several times between 1551 and 1704, and waited for something. India is superb at waiting.

An obviously disturbed man in his mid-thirties pressed his palm against St Faustina's image of Jesus with killer rays coming out of his heart. 'Jesus, I trust in you,' read the caption, and the man was repeating this over and over again. They were probably his only words of English. 'Paint an image according to the pattern you see, with the signature: "Jesus I trust in you,"' the Polish nun, Faustina, was told by God, according to her diary. 'I desire that this image be venerated, first in your chapel and then throughout the world. I promise that the soul that will venerate this image will not perish. I also promise victory over its enemies already here on earth, especially at the hour of death. I Myself will defend it as My own glory....'

That evening I dived into the colourful chaos of puja at a Shiva temple. Bells rang, drums thumped like my own heartbeat at the approach to the image in the hot damp dark; a beggar with no legs sat on a skateboard and scooted himself with one hand into the inner sanctuary; the other held a coconut to delight the Lord Shiva. A woman wept quietly as she walked up to the officiating priest. She carried a bowl of steaming rice; on the saucepan lid was a melting plastic doll representing the baby that she hoped the lingam of Shiva would give her. The tears stopped when the sandalwood paste touched her forehead, as if it had bored a hole through which the tormenting demons fled.

Bede Griffiths, at least at one stage, thought that Hinduism was bound to give way to Western rationalism; that as Indians qualified in accountancy and engineering they'd find incredible the idea of offering bananas to a lingam or an elephant-headed god. He wrote in 1955: 'I feel that as a religion, [Hinduism] is passing away. However strong it may be at the moment, it cannot survive the impact of modern thought which is undermining it on all sides.' It was a peculiarly imperceptive comment from a usually penetrating thinker. It denotes a failure to realise the immense psychological depths at which myth operates, and therefore a failure to recognise that in all cultures, everywhere, myth trumps history in the souls of the people. It is curious coming from a man who seems to have known that native gods can never be exorcised, but only baptised.

St Thomas sometimes took refuge in the Little Mount caves, not far from St Thomas' Mount. I met the merry nuns there again, and we all filed into a cave beneath the chapel. One of the nuns handed me a mint and a torch, and I obediently looked at the places she pointed to. The sign outside told me what I was seeing: 'Inside the caves one could see a boulder that clearly shows the impression of a huge foot, and near to that a finger impression and blood stain. It is the impression of [the] Saint's own hands which touched the wounds of Lord Jesus. The impression is far from artificial and there is [a] plausible explanation for its size: that over the centuries rock grows.'

That night I sat in the Hotchips Veg Restaurant eating chickpeas and watching the bats dance like hot black snowflakes in the light from the sweatshop above. In my notebook (stained where a Syrian priest had sprinkled it with holy water to sanctify my words), I wrote:

'Christian historicity is only abandoned or incredibly supplemented when the Grand, Historical, True Myth is insufficiently ignited in the imagination. Properly lit, the Myth can warm those depths of the Unconscious normally kept comfortable by the myths of corn and snake gods. But it's far less dangerous to adore a saint's footprint than a theological principle. Any of my cherished theological principles is bound to have a large amount of *me* in it. I am the one thing that I know can't possibly save me.'

~

## Chapter 8

# TRAINS AND MYTHS

'How comes it that [the Psalms] lack something... something all-important, if we are endeavouring to assess their contemporary value as, let us say, a book of devotion? I mean the sense of the indwelling Spirit, of all that is implied in the word 'sacramental'. Once again we are brought face to face with the peculiar destiny of the Jewish nation. The gods were immanent in pagan and gentile souls, in the Midianites, the Hittites, the Perizzites and the Jebusites, in a way that they could never be, must never be, in the Jewish...'

— Owen Barfield
*The Psalms of David*

~

'Who sees all beings in his own Self, and his own Self in all beings, loses all fear. When a sage sees this great Unity, and his Self has become all beings, what delusion and what sorrow can ever be near him?'

— *Isa Upanishad*

~

At the railway station, the next day, the crowd parted, like the sea before Moses, before a fragrant, bouffant-haired American woman in her mid-sixties, and her posse of sweating porters. To my alarm she made a bee-line for me. She trusted me because I had just had one of my very occasional shaves. 'I take it that you are going to Madurai?' she boomed.

'No. To Trichy,' I replied. I felt as if I'd let her down, and she clearly felt the same.

'I see,' she said, and at the same time she saw my ragged trousers and disreputable boots. It was probably the only time that she'd ever doubted her own first impression of anything. Doubt wasn't really her thing.

'Watch my bags, will you?' she commanded, and without waiting for an answer strode off to buy a newspaper. She returned ten minutes later, loudly disgusted that they didn't have the *Herald Tribune*. Her porters lugged her disc-rupturing Samsonite luggage into the First Class air-conditioned carriage, and she paid them in dollars, in sums that must have destabilised the local economy for miles around. The porters, assuming that she'd made a mistake and would soon realise it, galloped off down the platform and out of the station. She looked after them with distaste. 'Savages,' she muttered. She turned to me. I wasn't good, but I was the next best thing to the *Herald Tribune,* and she had wisdom to impart. 'This is a filthy place, isn't it,' she said, without a question mark. 'Hot, corrupt, primitive and depraved.'

'As a matter of fact,' I ventured bravely, 'I'm getting to love it all. But then that's probably because I'm filthy and depraved myself.'

Her face was like stone. 'Let me tell you, young man,' she said, not intending to flatter. 'I've seen things in the last few days which, if they happened in Iowa, would attract lengthy and well-deserved prison sentences for obscenity.'

'I haven't been so lucky,' I said, unwisely.

Her nose twitched, as if she'd caught the smell from my socks, which is possible. But she persevered. 'My driver stopped yesterday at some sort of outlandish roadside shrine. He said he had something to show me. I poked my head inside, and there they were. You know. The *things*. In marble.'

'I'm sorry?' I said, having a pretty good idea what she was talking about, but keen by now to maximise her discomfort.

She leant closer to me, looked around, and whispered, 'The organs. Of reproduction. His and hers. Disgusting. Repellent. No wonder this country is in such a bad way. Surely all the misery is just divine judgement for permitting such smut. And to have it in the centre of a religious monument. There simply are no words.' And there weren't. For either of us. Her outrage was profound, incurable and inexpressible. And I could see no way of telling her that the lingam of Shiva is a symbol of creative, life-giving power, and that the yoni indicates that power itself is not enough; reciprocity is at the root of creation. And so on. Her Iowan church no doubt taught her that the 'Song of Songs' has nothing at all to do with sex, that Solomon's concubines were actually secretaries employed to help him put erudite footnotes into his copy of the Torah, and that we know that Jesus never married because we know he didn't sin. But she did have six children.

As her train pulled out I saw her wagging a long, pale, jewelled finger at the impeccably polite conductor, presumably for being Indian in some respect.

On the train on the way to Trichy I dived again into Juan Mascaro's magnificent translation of the Upanishads. Whether or not they faithfully distil the essence of Hindu philosophy, they are the products of well-integrated men – powerful codifiers, adept in linear logic, but sublime poets and frontier-pushing mystics too. There have never been many such writers. Bede Griffiths concluded that the Conscious and Unconscious had met in these men. Their existence and their manner of writing gave him hope that a marriage of East and West was possible.

The earliest Upanishads were composed between 800 and 400 BC. Most of the Upanishads are later than the four Vedas – the foundational texts of Hinduism. The Vedas are hymns containing detailed accounts of Hindu mythology, passionate exhortations to religious observance, bleak verdicts on the irreligious, and dazzling, kaleidoscopic performances by writers schooled in ecstasy and close to the heart of joy. At their best the pages of the Vedas tremble at the footfall of the dancing Lord Shiva.

Literarily wonderful though they are, the Upanishads are rather sniffily middle class towards the Vedas. They see the Vedas as the province of the uneducated and unwashed peasants who would never dream of listening to Bach or reading the

*New York Review of Books*. They are plainly embarrassed that many Hindus take the colourful myths so literally, and want to put them right. The authors clearly regard themselves as having been favoured with special knowledge, which they might well have been.

In the Bhagavad Gita (which is really an Upanishad), the author dismissively comments: 'As is the use of a well of water where water everywhere overflows, such is the use of the Vedas to the seer of the Supreme.' The Svetasvatara Upanishad asks: 'Of what use is the Rig Veda to one who does not know the Spirit from whom the Rig Veda comes?' The clear implication here is that the writer of the Upanishad *does* know the spirit and will, if read obediently, tell his horny-handed, numskulled readers how to appropriate it.

The authors of the Upanishads were religious revisionists. They were the early Cromwells of the Hindu world, and they strode through India in their immaculate white dhotis metaphorically but systematically smashing up the idols of the Hinduism that they saw as outdated and primitive. Often they preached about the 'spiritual' or philosophical meanings of the old myths, in much the same way as a liberal Christian commentator might talk about the 'spiritual' nature of Jesus' resurrection, while denying its historicity. And sometimes, plainly thinking that myth was an inevitable vehicle for a particular truth, but that the existing myth was beyond the pale, they would compose alternative myths, purportedly more complete or coherent than the old. The Prasna Upanishad, for instance, has its own brand new creation myth, and its own new myth explaining how life comes to and is sustained in the body.

Actually, whatever the Upanishads were doing, it was always a form of myth making. Bede was wrong in thinking that the authors bridged the worlds of myth and reason. The explicit weavers of new myths were just being more honest, more realistic and wiser than the spiritualisers and philosophisers. The spiritualisers and philosophisers simply make one of the conceivable meanings of the myths more accessible to those members of the educated elite who can understand their language. They necessarily have to deploy the language of mystery, every cadence of which is the child and spawner of myth. The new, synthetic myths are less potent, less colourful and less multivalent than the old ones, which surged up straight from the source. And they are far less accessible to the rank and file peasantry of India and, increasingly, to me. Give me wild Vedic Hinduism any day instead of the slightly self-satisfied University Hinduism of the Upanishads. If you really want to get in touch with the Unconscious, it's better to do it directly rather than negotiate with it through an agent in a smart New Delhi office. Things get distorted when they are filtered through third parties. The Chinese Whispers principle works in theology as well as at children's parties. The Upanishads are an ancient attempt to produce a sort of systematic theology of Hinduism. All attempts to produce a systematic theology of any serious religion are doomed, and often the religion itself suffers, sometimes to death, in the process of attempted encapsulation.

I finished the Upanishads, put them in my rucksack, took out my battered copy of the Rig Veda, and immediately spilt chickpea curry over Parjanya, the cow. 'All worlds rest on him,' I read, through the spreading yellow stain, 'the triple skies and the triple flowing waters. The three vats that drench pour forth in all directions the overflowing honey.'

India rumbled away beneath me. Bee-eaters chattered on the scrub bushes, and buffaloes ploughed the paddies. The compartment was packed. I was squeezed against the window, and people were snoring in the luggage racks above my head. I wrote. I looked up to see every neck craned and every eye following every word in my notebook. Nobody in the carriage spoke a word of English, and they certainly couldn't follow my writing (I barely can myself), but the absorption was complete. I looked around each of them, and smiled. They held my gaze, but none smiled back at me. I could think of no real reason why they should. I went on writing, and all the eyes returned to my pen.

Nobody in that carriage spoke English, but there was someone on the train who did. A clean-shaven Indian man in his mid-thirties, dressed in a shiny business suit and carrying a briefcase far too thin to be useful, made the effort of coming all the way from the first class compartment to the second class to say, angrily but elegantly, with a bow: 'Excuse me, sir. I think you are from England?'

I nodded. 'I am indeed.'

'I thought so. The trousers gave you away. "Genteel scruffiness", I believe, you call it. Against you I bear no ill will. You are most welcome here, and I hope that you are enjoying your stay and will return many times, but I swore to my grandfather that I would tell every Englishman that I met that, despite what you might think, you contributed nothing to this country but misery. You have nothing to teach us. Would you please tell that to the missionaries who are now seeking to turn our poor, vulnerable people from the faith of their ancestors to their Western beliefs and alien values? You have nothing to teach us. And now, goodbye, and have a pleasant journey through Tamil Nadu and through life.'

He bowed again and went back to the first class compartment.

I resented nothing about this, except the suggestion that there's anything genteel about my trousers. But it set me thinking.

As the train pulled into Maduranthakam, I decided that the question of Christianity's contribution to India was too hard for someone as underslept as I was, and I went to sleep. The sidings outside Villupuram jolted me awake, and I felt alive enough to start thinking instead about whether Hinduism had anything to contribute to Christianity. Yes, I'd decided, by the time we arrived at Vriddhachalam. Absolutely, yes. A few miles outside Tiruchirapalli (Trichy) I'd concluded that its contribution is not what it is usually thought to be. And also, to my surprise, I found that the train of thought led inexorably on to a conclusion to the initial question: has Christianity anything unique to contribute? The route that train took was this.

Hinduism is the most detailed religious exposition of the life of the Unconscious that there is. No one who looks at it properly can fail to be awed by its virility, poetry and power; can fail to be thrilled at the sound of the resonant chords it strikes in deep places – often places we were unaware existed in us at all. In Hinduism we hear the sound of one hand clapping, and it is an exhilarating sound. Its nature-gods are the ones that we should all long to worship, and at some level do worship. The gods speak with golden lips of a time when we were not so painfully dislocated from the natural world, and their propitiation seems to offer a direct route to reconciliation with it.

When Westerners turn their backs on the arid, autistic churches of Europe and the US, and flock to the ashrams of India, they all say, at least at first, that they have come home. It's quite something for a German accountant, fresh from Chennai airport, to be at home in the company of vengeful, multi-armed and animal-headed gods. What can it mean?

It means that Hinduism is awakening in him long-dormant and probably actively suppressed memories of a wild, unfettered time, long overwhelmed by spreadsheets, calculations, corporate brown-nosing and the stern imperatives of commercial selfishness. When he goes into the ashram's temple he knows that he has been missing something that matters hugely; that is central to life as a human being; that is essential for joy. Ganesh first whispers and then trumpets to his Unconscious, and slowly it starts to awake.

All this is good. The danger comes when one colossal error (the West's absurd insistence that the rational and material are all there is), is replaced by another (Hinduism's much more understandable insistence that the Unconscious is all there is: that reality is illusion; that we and everything else are simply thoughts in the mind of Brahman). Let the Unconscious out, unchecked, and the end is madness, which is neither philosophically rewarding nor fun.

The madness of the untrammelled rule of the Unconscious, though, seems to me to be less sinister than the opposing madness of Western rationalism – particularly when that rationalism is dressed up in religious clothes. Who's nearer to what they are meant to be: a raving ashramite, grappling miserably and unsuccessfully with demons as he sits cross-legged in the meditation hall, or a black-coated Ulsterman heaving a brick through a Catholic shop window in order to point out the theological superiority of his beliefs about transubstantiation?

Hinduism can and should *remind* the Christians what their faith is meant to be about. Probably most worthwhile learning is actually *anamnesis*: unforgetting. Hinduism can help to remind everyone, eloquently and beautifully, that there's a massive part of ourselves which we neglect at our peril, and which Christianity has neglected to its peril. It's a detailed map of the seething Unconscious; of the raging sea of the psyche; of the myths from which we can never escape. It's the book of the elemental.

But a book that reignites old and precious memories of

childhood won't necessarily be a completely satisfactory blueprint for the whole of life.

I put down my pen and gazed out of the window. We had stopped opposite a paddy-field. A crow ripped a tick from a buffalo's ear. It burst the tick as it did so, and blood spurted into the crow's eyes.

The man with the slimline briefcase had come back from the first class compartment, and leant against the door, watching me. 'There was one thing I should have said,' he started. 'I see that you are writing. I've no idea what you are writing, but don't bother. You cannot understand anything about India, and it's arrogant to think that you can. Once again, good luck, and goodbye.'

'Goodbye,' I murmured. He turned and left, and I went back to the ludicrously big question I'd posed. Can anything be a 'satisfactory blueprint' for something as majestic as the whole of a human life?

The answer, obviously, was no. Existence is far too big, colourful and complex to be capable of being governed by any statement of belief. The greatest Christian creeds have explicitly recognised this, acknowledging the inevitability of invoking wholly non-propositional language – and so the dismal inadequacy of language and accordingly creeds themselves. The Athanasian Creed tells us about 'the Father incomprehensible, the Son incomprehensible, and the Holy Spirit incomprehensible. The Father eternal, the Son eternal, and the Holy Spirit eternal. And yet they are not three eternals but one eternal. As also there are not three uncreated nor three incomprehensible, but one uncreated and one incomprehensible.' It's magnificent, and curiously convincing, because the use of such language means that the author recognises that his task as a verbal encapsulator of the Universe's deepest mysteries is utterly hopeless.

All great creeds end by asserting that creeds won't do. That's what you'd expect. If they can't even tell us satisfactorily what God is like, they are bound to fail to tell us adequately how to relate to Him, Her, Them or It. After all, to live at all as a human being is itself a religious act. There's nothing we can do that is not sacramental. Words are important, but they are bound to be insufficient. If words adequately capture your god, your god is far too small to be God. This is true for scripture as well as for creeds, as Jesus' contempt for Pharisaism dramatically illustrated. What mischief has been done by Luther's journalistic strap line, 'Sola scriptura'? Has any similar advertising jingle or sound bite ever been so consistently and disastrously worshipped and misconstrued?

Canonical scripture is 'God-breathed', writes the unknown author of not-St-Paul's Second Letter to Timothy – referring presumably to the Old Testament, because there wasn't a New one then. The Iowan evangelical who disliked my trousers no doubt used the verse whenever she told anyone how much God hates gays. But God had and has other breaths apart from the ones he may have used to inspire, so inconsistently, the many draftsmen and editors of the Bible. You're trying to derive from the Bible the notion that you need only the Bible for wisdom and knowledge of God? Don't bother: it can't be done. It was never meant to be done.

The train hadn't moved. There were flowers like foam on a tree that touched the window. A mantis stalked a butterfly, and missed. An old man on the seat opposite me unrolled the banana leaf that held his lunch. The train jerked on, catapulting all his rice onto his lap and then, with a second jolt, onto the floor. He sighed, brushed himself down, and took out a lavishly illustrated Tamil textbook of animal trapping.

If one is looking for a *system* for living, seeking meaning and relating to God, myth is very obviously a much more satisfactory medium than the most cunningly drafted set of propositions – hence the incantatory magnetism of Hinduism for anyone who has discovered the inadequacy of creeds (surely all right thinking people with any experience at all of the world).

The obvious first thought is syncretism – a happy marriage of Christianity and Hinduism, in which Hinduism helps Christianity to discover its feminine side, and Christianity gives Hinduism some lessons in morality, ethics and order, and a mechanism for achieving the redemption that we all long for. The Cross seems intuitively more satisfactory a solution to the problem of alienation from God than offering a rice pudding to a ceramic statue. It's dramatic, bloody, and costly enough, and is designed to produce reconciliation at all levels. I can see that the rice pudding works at some levels. It's hard to see how it works cosmically. I can see that

Christianity might (although it has signally failed to do in almost all Christian cultures) rip up the veil separating the conscious and the unconscious, and let those two parts of life inform and serenade one another. History tells, though, that one of the frequent errors of Christian-Hindu syncretism is to think that this is all that it does – that this reconciliation is the whole business of redemption. Do that, and you empty Christianity of its crucial moral content. You can't coherently identify the unconscious with sin, assert that the unconscious is the source of all sin, or think that a little infusion of reason is all that is necessary to sanctify the demonic unconsciousness.

There's another practical reason why syncretism doesn't work. Too often it's not a merger, but a take-over by the Unconscious. This isn't surprising; any merger has to be on the basis that each party has something to offer, and Christian-Hindu mergers are generally on the basis that Christianity can bring only order and laughably inadequate credal propositions, and is wholly incompetent when it comes to the Unconscious. They are approached on the basis of an analogy to the British in India: the Christians are the stiff-shirted emotional retards who build good railways; the Hindus are the ones with the real, enduring wisdom, who might nonetheless benefit from travelling on the railways in order to visit distant temples. Put like this (and Christians should hang their heads in shame because it can very convincingly be put like this), what chance does Christianity have in such a partnership? How can a credal proposition stand against ecstasy? Against the surging poetry of the sea? Against the virile gods of harvest and river? Against sex and sun and the throb of drums in the dark?

If creeds don't work (and in any event cater to only one half — the reasonable half — of any human being), if pure myth is deadly when allowed to run wild (and in any event caters only to the other half of any human), and if syncretism ends in the unfettered rule of myth, what can help to make us whole humans? There's only one possibility left: a personal *relationship* with the Reality towards which all religious systems grope, to which all myths more or less dimly allude.

'I'm back, I'm afraid,' said the man with the slimline briefcase. 'I said that you are welcome. I have now reflected, and regret that that is not true. I think you should leave India. In the meantime you should abandon the pose of travelling second class, and come up to the first class compartment, where you will contaminate fewer Indians.'

'Get out,' I said, standing up. 'Get out and don't come back.'

He stared at me very hard for a long time, looked round at the others in the carriage, who were transfixed, turned abruptly on his expensive heels, and left.

There are many problems with the possibility of a personal relationship with Reality. It assumes that Reality has a personality; that Reality wants to have a relationship with us; and that Reality, the Ground of all Being, which was there before the Big Bang, which conjured colour out of the dark, hurled stars into the deep cold, and shaped the wings of humming birds, is capable of making itself sufficiently accessible to fragile, transient creatures. Presumably the ability to understand is to some extent a function of experience: if that is so, what hope have we of understanding anything of a Creator? Our lifespan in comparison to the age of the Universe is fantastically shorter than that of a gnat to ours. Yet one can have no relationship without accessibility and some sort of mutual understanding. It all seems a pretty tall order.

If Christian creeds themselves acknowledge their own inadequacy and incoherence, on what basis can it sensibly be said that Christianity is in any sense a more rational religion than, for instance, Hinduism? Hinduism contributes a matchlessly detailed account of the myths that drive our psyches. Has Christianity, so apparently deficient in the myth-market, and by the admission of its top creed-draftsmen so obviously incapable of systemising its own religious claims, anything at all to bring to the party?

I don't know, but I can only understand its claims like this: Christianity's claims to rationalism can only mean that its claims are in some way accessible to tiny human minds. It means, in fact, that Christians claim that God made himself available to be touched, joked with, eaten with, spat at, flogged and nailed to a piece of wood. And all in the same space and time dimension through which we process, and all in a way accessible to ordinary, unspiritual, unenlightened eyes. When Christianity says it's reasonable, what it's really saying is that Jesus was historical and that the resurrection happened in precisely the same sense as the collision happened between two biryani salesman at the platform the train was standing at when I wrote this.

In identifying the requirements of a workable religion, catering for both sides of the brain, and the claims that Christianity makes for itself, one simply cannot avoid the word 'accessible'. I've reluctantly used it several times myself in the last few paragraphs, being unable to think of a decent alternative. This might be significant.

A historical Jesus, an actual, verifiable resurrection, God making himself available for cross-examination by us – there's the reasonableness; there's the left brain stuff. But is there any myth? Well, if the Christians are right, it's *all* myth. The story of Jesus is the story of the dying and rising Balder, Dionysus and Osiris. The difference for the Christians is that his is the *true* myth, the one that the others were hinting at and looking forward to. They were the shadows on the Platonic wall – he was the figure in the sun. Bacchus existed in the minds of his priests and people, and somewhere in the collective unconscious. Jesus existed in the Temple, inns and backstreets of Jerusalem, and died at the hands of the Roman authorities at the age of about thirty-three. But here's the thing: in Christianity the conscious, reasonable element and the wild, mythical element turn out not simply to be united in some sort of partnership. They are the same thing. They are both Jesus of Nazareth. We don't have the sort of marriage of East and West that Bede Griffiths dreamed of; we have a complete *identity* of East and West.

Christianity is meant to be a celebration of *wholeness*. Jesus, say the Christians, was the supreme example of the whole man. It wasn't that he was an amphibian, capable of living equally happily in the rational and the unconscious, in the left brain and the right brain. He lived all the time, and lived fully, in both. He never said anything that was merely reasonable or merely intuitive. If he read a physics textbook, he would do it with the ecstasy of a lover reading a letter from a long-estranged beloved. He was a poet without peer, but without a syllable of obscurity. His most tear-jerking, soul-wrenching stanzas were all sublimely reasonable. In every sentence is the passion of the eye of the storm and the power of a mountainous wave. But the storm is never allowed to destroy, or the wave to drown.

The train pulled into Trichy. Slimline Briefcase was met and hugged on the platform by his adoring mother. He waved and smiled at me as I walked out of the station.

～

## Chapter 9

# ON THE BANKS OF A RIVER

'I know that Great Person of the brightness of the sun beyond
the darkness.
Only by knowing Him one goes beyond death.
There is no other way to go.'

                  – *Svetasvatara Upanishad*

~

'The Father and I are one.'

                  – *John 10: 30*

~

It was with all this swirling in my head that I arrived at
Shantivanam. It was the worst possible frame of mind in which
to arrive.

Saccidananda Ashram, at Shantivanam, is outside the little
village of Kullittalai, on the south bank of the sacred river
Cauvery – the Ganges of south India. It was established in
1950 by two Benedictine monks who wore round their necks

the Benedictine cross with, in the centre, the *pronava* – a symbol of God the Eternal Word springing out of silence. It was an affirmation that the historical Christ was and is Brahman. The name 'Saccidananda' asserts, even more forcefully, that Christianity and Hinduism are merely different perspectives on one truth. The word is Sanskrit – the ancient liturgical language of India – and it combines three elements, 'Sat', 'Cit' and 'Ananda', which are generally rendered 'Being', 'Thought' and 'Bliss' respectively. It's common to hear Western commentators say that these are 'attributes' of deity. They are not; deity *is* these things. It's an uncomfortable distinction, but one worth wrestling with. Perhaps the most important thing, though, is how the conjoined word 'Saccidananda' is translated: it is, to howls of protest by most orthodox Christians, translated as 'Holy Trinity'.

The banana leaves swelled gradually all the way south from Chennai. By the time I got to Shantivanam (the 'forest of peace') they were monstrous. They blocked the view of the great Ranganathaswamy temple that rears out of the plain, dappled the lumpily deformed arms of the Ambassador taxi driver, and pushed aggressively towards the doors of all the little ceramic temples along the road, as if they wanted to be first in the queue for blessing. You feel the competition for temple colour and temple size between neighbouring villages. They are a lot more interesting than the thatched huts in which everyone lives. Regardless of my theology, if I lived in one of those villages, my *eyes* would want to go to the temple everyday for some relief. The temple statues speak too of epic possibility in a world where there's no possibility at all. Their attraction at all levels must be immense.

The ashram is a well-regulated riot of numbered trees and well-managed shrubs. Iridescent humming-birds and butterflies circle the honey-suckle clockwise at the same pace, as if there's some Edenic agreement between them. No level is wasted. On the ground there are useful herbs and incongruous, gratuitous roses. At eye level are blazing flowers, cascading out of their leaves; then vertiginous palms; and then the blue, cut by swifts.

The car dropped me at the tea-circle, where the community meets to chat, and an old Indian man with a puja-mark beckoned me over and motioned me to sit and drink water. Soon I was bustled away by a business-like house-manager woman with a splendid green sari and limited but very gentle English. She asked me my 'God-name', said that I could order some made-to-measure pyjamas for 350 rupees, showed me to my room, and told me that tea would be at half past three.

There was nothing bogus at Shantivanam, and no pretensions. It seemed happy in its own skin. At first this looked like diffidence. I was neither ignored nor interrogated. If I wanted to speak, people wanted to listen. If I wanted to be silent, people wanted to be silent too. There was a palpable peace here. 'There's none of the frantic ego-trippery of the other ashrams,' said Helga, a forty-five-year-old Austrian, who ought to know. 'None of the spiritual masturbation.'

Whatever the reason for that peace, it's not Christian orthodoxy.

After tea, we all filed into the meditation room, where, for an hour, we could ask questions of Brother Martin, the head monk. He was an Indian Camaldolese monk, brought up in Andhra Pradesh, who had become first a disciple of Bede Griffiths and then the inheritor of his mantle. He was kind, with a bit of a paunch and a reassuring lack of charisma. It surprised me when he sat in a blue plastic chair while we all sat cross-legged on the floor in front of him. It was a bit too guru-esque or priestly for me, but I don't think it was meant like that. He generally didn't seem to like sitting on the floor. The plastic chair was probably a consequence of arthritis or piles rather than theology.

It surprised me, too, when he purported to give *answers*. Only later did it occur to me that I was being unfair, and he gave answers mainly because he was being asked questions. There was certainly no lack of humility: I suppose I expected the responses to be more shruggingly amorphous than they were, and the format to be more a sharing of travellers' tales than a seminar. I later read that Brother Martin had said, 'For me, personally, I have no more questions', and liked him less. He had a little black board at his side, on which he chalked up alarmingly definite solutions to the problems posed.

The theological algebra was sometimes curious. 'What is the Self?' asked a thin, earnest Indian who had known Bede Griffiths and who spent his life on another Christian ashram near Mylapore.

'Whatever it is,' replied Brother Martin, without hesitation, 'it must have two qualities. It must have unity, and it must be timeless.' Nobody asked 'why?' or 'unity with what?'

'Thus I cannot be merely a body,' he went on. 'A body is not timeless. I cannot be merely a set of personal characteristics, for they are not timeless either. They will dissipate when my body rots. I cannot be merely a member of my village, or an Indian, or a Catholic, or a Christian. That would mean that I did not have unity with people outside my village, or with non-Indians, non-Catholics or non-Christians. Nor can it mean that I am a human being. That would mean that I was not in unity with the rest of creation — animals, plants and so on. Nor can it mean that I am a creature. That would mean I had no unity with God. So what can it mean? It can only mean that my Self is God.' He chalked up the 'equals' sign on the board, and looked satisfied.

There wasn't actually a ripple of applause from the floor, but it felt as if there should have been. A white-haired Californian woman nodded hard. The earnest Indian smiled gently. But Brother Martin hadn't quite finished. 'The problem,' he said, 'is that we think of ourselves as individuals. That's what does the harm and creates the confusion.'

I couldn't keep quiet at this, but wasn't clear where to start. 'Jesus had a resurrection body,' I ventured. 'We're told that we'll have one too. Doesn't that imply that we've got, and are meant eternally to have, some sort of discrete identity? There's no point in having a body unless it's distinct from other bodies; feeling different things; wanting different things; *being* a different thing.'

Brother Martin didn't pause, but the answer was no answer at all. 'Ah well,' he said, 'there's a sense in which individuality is still retained. The resurrection of our body means the awakening of the eternal reality in us. That will be experienced in different ways in each person.'

'But was the tomb empty on the Third Day?' I asked, feeling rude and cheap.

Again, no answer, but this time a long discourse. 'There are many ways in which we can understand the resurrection. We tend to put truth in a tomb. The resurrection shows that it won't stay there. It bursts out. Or, again, it's a sort of childbirth. The tomb is the womb of religion. Human beings have to be expelled from that womb. Jesus' resurrection showed that he escaped the womb; he transcended religion and therefore history – so demonstrating his unity with the eternal reality which is beyond all religion. It's the victory of the Eternal Present over the past, present and future. It's a victory over the tyranny of historical truth.'

'Tyranny?' I protested. 'History's our medium, isn't it? History matters to me. It's in history that I eat and laugh and live and die. And doesn't it matter to God too? The Incarnation shows that history matters; time matters; flesh and blood matter.'

Like so many people in India to whom I'd talked, he looked slightly tired. 'We think that only because our perspective is very limited. From where we are the earth seems flat, although we know it's not.'

'But the whole notion of a beginning and a coming Kingdom, both inescapable in Judaism and Christianity, are only compatible with God's primary revelation to us being in history,' I went on, boring or alarming the others. 'Even if God hadn't specifically endorsed time as one of the main dimensions in which to construct his relationship with us, could we conceivably relate to him otherwise? Isn't trying to understand the world using the model of *advaita* (non-duality) as hopeless as commissioning a fish to live in the Sahara, or for Piscean intellectuals to write a geography of Everest?'

Brother Martin was much more patient and gracious than I was. He listened quietly. We both knew that we had started to argue, and there was the unmistakable sight of an approaching blind alley. I thought that he didn't understand, and he thought that I didn't. I stopped, bowed, and went back to my room.

A boy walked deliberately toward the table in the garden where I was writing. He stopped, raised his hand, and said, 'Hello. What are you doing?' 'I'm writing,' I said. He smiled, completely satisfied, raised his hand again, and turned to walk away the way he had come.

Two egrets flew over the dry bed of the Cauvery. A falcon came like a spear from the sun, so fast that it seemed to leave a black trail behind it. The lead egret crumpled as it was hit, tumbling onto the sand. A white feather rocked down like a boat, bearing a single bead of blood. The air was so hot that the blood was dry by the time I walked over to it. The other egret beat on to the other bank.

Morning, noon and night, the worship began with the Gayatri Mantra, chanted three times. The first 'Om' came out of an immense and ancient silence, and was the sound of that silence. The consonants were shocking.

> *Om bhur bhuva svaa*
> *Tat savitur varenyam*
> *Bhargo devasaya dhimahi*
> *Dhiyo yo nam prachchodyat*

*Salutations to the Word, which is present in the earth, the sky and that which is beyond. Let us meditate on the glorious splendour of that divine Giver of Life. May he illuminate our meditation.*

In the morning, as the sun began to unfold the wings of the swallowtails, and the palm swifts began to hunt the aerial plankton in the first air spirals, we prayed:

> *Om: may all the world be happy.*
> *Om: from the unreal lead me to the real, from darkness lead me to light, from death lead me to immortality.*
> *Om: that is full, this is full, from fullness, fullness proceeds; removing fullness from fullness, fullness alone remains.*
> *Om: peace, peace, peace.*

At noon, when the heat struck the peacocks silent, the Cauvery sand shivered, and the sun drove away all shadow, flattening the land, we sang:

> *Lord of the Universe, O eternal consciousness, I bow to you.*
> *Most Holy, O Supreme Spirit, forever and ever I bow to you.*
> *We worship the true God who is the Supreme Being, who is fragrant,*
> *and who nourishes all beings. May He liberate us from death, even*
> *as a cucumber is severed from its bondage to the creeper.*

And at night, when the bats started to flicker round the trees, the crows went quietly to roost above the funeral pyre, and the crickets made the forest throb, the refrain was ecstatic and almost manic, piling title, adjective, superlative, image, metaphor and concept crazily on top of each other in a strained, failed effort to praise the ineffable enough:

> *Glory to Sacchidananda, the Existent, the Knower, the blissful, the*
> *furthest goal, despised by the world, longed for by saints, the*
> *Almighty, the ancient, the fullness, the undivided, higher than the*
> *highest, the far and the near, related within, pure and unrelated*
> *without, the aware, whom intellect scarce can reach. The Father,*
> *the inciter, the unbegotten, the great Lord, the cause of all; the*
> *seedless seed of the tree of being, from whose regard all this proceeds;*
> *the protector of the world. The uncreated Son, the Word without end,*
> *the great Person, the image of the Father, the essential wisdom, the*
> *Saviour. The blessed, the essential Joy, proceeding from the unity of*
> *Being and Consciousness, the sanctifier, the swift, the revealer of*
> *the revealing Son, the giver of life. Glory to Sacchidananda.*

Having reached out with the entire lexicon, and fallen dismally short, we walked silently out into the dark to look for other ways.

Although in the liturgy he invoked a 'holy' God several times a day, Brother Martin was uncomfortable with the idea of holiness. Holiness is about separation, about a God who is *other*. This, he thought, was an unhelpful vestige of Hebrew thought which Jesus had made redundant. 'I and the Father are one,' was the phrase to which Brother Martin constantly returned. 'It indicates that Jesus had entered the Unitary Consciousness,' he said. 'That Individual Consciousness had been emptied completely, leaving only God.'

He thought that Jesus was saying nothing new. 'He was not saying anything that wasn't already in the Vedic tradition. When he said "I and the Father are one", he was actually elevating his spiritual tradition to the highest of the Upanishadic sayings. It was the first time that this statement was made in the Prophetic tradition, but this statement was made five-hundred years before Christ in the Upanishads, when the sages said, "I am Brahman", or "I am God". In the Christian tradition, this expression has been suppressed for theological reasons, because Christianity believes in a Creator God. In Christianity, it is not possible for human beings to make this statement, the exception is made for Jesus Christ.'

Well, yes. This exposition of Hinduism's idea of advaita is at odds with the whole Hebrew tradition; at odds with the notion that God created, and is distinct from his creatures; at odds with the ethos of the prophetic tradition, in which a people distinct from their God have constantly to be called back to him; at odds with the whole bloody history of sacrifice, and the explicit continuity of Jesus' life and death with the whole sacrificial pattern. Abolish otherness, and you are at least half way towards abolishing morality. It's hard to accommodate ethical demands within the structure of advaita. Who in the advaitic world is able to insist, prescribe and proscribe?

In his writings, Brother Martin is very frank about this. He acknowledges the difficulty that he had with the notion that Jesus died for our sins, so saving mankind. He has come to the conclusion that it's to be understood like this: 'Christ had an experience of God that transcended the experience of God possible in his spiritual tradition. Christ's experience was a revolution because it inaugurated the New Covenant in which human beings (and not religion) had become the centre. This experience put his spiritual tradition in crisis. In the old relationship with God, the law and the Temple were absolute, but Christ made these two relative. In doing so, Christ became a threat to the whole Jewish tradition, so they accused him of blasphemy. Blasphemy was a sin that was punishable by death. Through the way he lived his life, Christ said, "Yes, the experience is real for me and it is possible for everybody, and I'm standing by it. If you want to kill me, you kill me. I am ready to die, but I am not going to take back my stand." That is the reason why Christ had to die. We have to be clear about it.'

So for Brother Martin, Jewish tradition was wrong. Jewish history was not a process in which God educated the Jews correctly in how to relate to him, but a tragic process in which the Jews had got hold of completely the wrong end of the stick. Jesus, abandoning everything Judaism taught him, and insisting on the advaitic wisdom of India, suffered the fate that many ground-breaking visionaries suffer at the hands of fearful conservatives.

But Jesus does not look like that to me. He looks more Jewish every time I look at him. He even looked that way on the banks of the Cauvery. He was emphatically a dualist; even he, the son, was distinct from his father. The Christians say that there is distinction even within the Trinity; it's a crucial prerequisite of relationship. Jesus spoke about the need for atonement; for bridge building; for reconciliation; of restored relationship with a Creator, not of identification with him. If you want an Indian Jesus, don't you have to forget that he was Bar Mitzvahed and murdered in Jerusalem?

To be fair to Shantivanam, there's no dishonest attempt to liberalise Christianity into conformity with the Upanishads. The technique is the straightforward use of the blue pencil. Where something in the Bible is inconvenient, it is simply deleted. At every service, the community uses 'Psalms for Christian Worship'. The title should raise eyebrows and suspicions. It has a long and illuminating introduction by Bede Griffiths:

'...as we come to attend more closely to the literal meaning of the psalms, which for an educated person today is almost inevitable, it becomes more and more difficult to accept many of them as Christian prayers. Taken in their literal sense many of the psalms express feelings of anger, hatred and revenge against one's enemies which are entirely opposed to the teaching of the gospel on love of one's enemies, and the habit of labelling a whole class of one's fellow men as "enemies", "wicked" and "sinners" is intolerable for anyone who has been taught to "love one's neighbours as oneself". What is perhaps even more unacceptable, the same sentiments of anger, hatred and revenge are attributed to God himself, and the Messiah in the famous Messianic psalms (2 and 109) is depicted as a King who will conquer and destroy his enemies, trampling them under his feet... In this the Messiah is shown to be the very opposite of Jesus Christ who allowed his enemies to crush him and came not to destroy but to save.'

Everyone who has read the vindictive Psalms will agree that there's a difficulty. But how should one deal with the difficulty? Bede goes on:

'It has become urgent, therefore, to revise the Psalter, so that all branding of others as "enemies", "wicked" and "sinners" deserving no mercy or pity should be removed. When one considers the incalculable harm which has resulted from this habit of mind in the church as seen in the Inquisition, the crusades, the wars of religion and the persecution of "heretics", it is clear that a revision of this kind is urgently needed.'

Weren't the Inquisition, the crusades, the wars of religion and the persecution of "heretics" a consequence of precisely the failure to acknowledge and grapple with the complexity of scripture that Bede's suggested solution displays? Why, in Bede's eyes, did Israel get it so badly wrong? For exactly the reasons indicated by Brother Martin:

'We have to remember that ancient Israel grew up in a dualistic culture in which God was considered to be separate – the word "holy" originally meant separate – from humanity and the created world. Human beings were separate from God and one another and from the surrounding world. Israel was a "holy" nation, separate from the other nations of the world. As a result, Israel was surrounded by "enemies" who were hostile to God and to the people of God. The good separate from the "wicked"; the righteous from sinners; and the end was conceived to be the destruction of the "wicked" and all the "enemies" of Israel, and the Messiah was to conquer their enemies and subdue them under his feet. This was the perspective of the Psalmist, and it was precisely this dualism which Jesus came to overcome. He broke down the dividing wall between Jews and Gentiles. He came not to conquer and subdue his enemies but to save them and reconcile them with God. He came to save not the "righteous" but sinners. Thus the whole perspective of the psalms in their literal sense is to perpetuate what Jesus came to bring to an end. There is, however, another side to the tradition of Israel, a sense of universalism, a recognition of the mercy and grace of God towards sinners. These psalms still retain their value and can be used in Christian prayers. These psalms retain all their value for Christian prayer when they have been separated from every suggestion of anger and hatred and revenge and be seen to lead to reconciliation in Christ of all humanity and the whole creation.'

It is too simple and too presumptuous. As for me, I'd rather read the terrible, unexpurgated psalms, writhing with embarrassment and discomfort; trying and failing to reconcile the stern tribal War-God of Israel with the God who washed feet and fried fish; recognising with alarm and disgust that the imperfect men and flawed poets chosen to write these hymns thought the same things about their enemies as I do about mine; realising that somehow the writhing takes me further up and further in than the blue pencil would.

There are few braver writers and explorers than Bede Griffiths. His humility and basic goodness ooze from every paragraph. He wanted to *know,* and, much more than that, he wanted to *encounter;* to relate; to be known. He pushed on and on when the rest of us have long lost our nerve. Those who met him said that the first thing they noticed was that he was 'fully present' to them. They meant by this that, however busy he was, however mobbed by admirers and disciples, he gave all of himself to each listener. Each felt that Bede was interested in them more passionately than he had ever been interested in anyone or anything else. The tortured Austrian girl, Helga, felt this even though Bede was long dead. There was, she said, a peculiar peace in the little hut at Shantivanam where Bede lived and died – a peace that reached out and understood.

Bede's hut has been preserved just as it was when he died. There's no furniture apart from a basic bed, a small table and a chair. He rebuked himself for never being able to dispense with these. It was at that table, looking out into the palm grove and the banana plantation beyond, that he carried on his astonishingly fecund correspondence with his old Oxford tutor, C.S. Lewis, and hundreds of seekers. It was in that bed that he had the stroke that, he said, literally shut down the male side of his brain enough to let the feminine take the part in him that it had always been longing to do. He felt a crushing pressure in his head. The pressure, he was convinced, came from the left and propelled his brain towards the right – towards the feminine, intuitive side. He felt compelled, as he put it, to 'surrender to the Mother'. Somehow he did. A wave burst over him. He cried out to a friend nearby, 'I'm being overwhelmed by love.' And so it seemed to everyone who saw him afterwards. Even the most cynical said that he radiated holiness, that he had been transfigured. Perhaps it was a curious way for a celibate monk to prepare for death, or perhaps it is what celibacy is all about.

As his coffin was lowered into the ground, the sky darkened and a strong wind blew. They say that his body refused to decompose, that the trees bowed reverentially towards his grave, and that flowers filled it.

He had long recognised the imbalance in himself and in the world. As a young, reflective priest he had bemoaned the suppression in himself of the female, the intuitive, the naturally sympathetic and empathetic. He ascribed the suppression partly to the stiff middle-class England in which he had been brought up, but later came to lay some of the blame for England's intrinsic patriarchal autism on its

Christianity. He knew that suppressed things are never fully suppressed – they always make themselves known, for good or ill. He feared what the suppressed feminine would do, and desired passionately its emancipation. This was his life's quest. Presumably because of the perceived extent of the suppression of the feminine in himself, he increasingly tended to use 'the feminine' and 'the Unconscious' as synonyms. This explains some of the imbalance in his writings. When he landed in India, he was intoxicated by the sight, smell and taste of the Unconscious in the bazaars, the eyes and the temple bells. He was romantically in love with India, with the Unconscious, with the idea of salvaging the tender parts of his childhood from his own Unconscious, with the Feminine, and with the Intuitive. And latterly he never really distinguished between these things. At the start of his Indian life, he warned himself sternly that the Unconscious was not the whole story; that it needed to be kept in its place. In a 1955 letter he wrote:

'I am rather afraid of the intuitive power becoming too dominant: don't you think that there is a danger of the unconscious *swamping* the conscious? I find that I have to go back again and again to simple Christian doctrine, to sin and repentance, grace and redemption, faith and self-surrender. If I allow myself to swell too much in Eastern thought I find it unbalances me, and I have to go back to the New Testament...'

He seems to have forgotten the warning, or lost the fear. In his later years he begged to be swamped. Perhaps it happened, as death approached. And perhaps the real challenge is to learn how to allow India to *irrigate* instead. But even if we can conclude that Bede got the balance wrong, the Western churches can draw no smugly comforting conclusions from it. Modern Christianity is hardly imperilled by the tyrannical rule of the ecstatic. Our dangers are not his. We're in no danger of drowning. We're in terrible danger of terminal desiccation, from which Bede was utterly safe. If I'm forced to opt for an error, I know which one I'd choose.

In the morning, as the villagers milk the cows, and the drums come along with the corpses to the bank of the river, and the first light cuts through the lacework of leaves above my room, we anoint ourselves with paste from sandalwood, as a sign of consecration. Its value speaks of divinity; its fragrance of grace. Even when the axe cuts into the trunk, it continues to give out its fragrance, and so it tells of the unconditional love of God.

At noon, as the blue smoke from the last of the body parts spirals up, collecting in a mushroom under the forest canopy, we use *kumkum* powder to drill the third, inner eye into our foreheads, the eye that sees the inner light. 'If your eye is single,' said Jesus, 'your whole body shall be full of light.'

In the evening, when the body-smoke has gone, and the Collared Scops Owl has begun to shrug and blink, we put ashes on our foreheads to remind us not only that we are dust, but also that our impurities have been burnt away, yet leaving something behind.

Morning, noon and night, fire is waved before the Sacrament to honour it and to reveal the Christ crouched hiding there. Then we scoop the fire into our faces, collect our shoes at the door, and leave.

'The fire here is *safe* fire,' said Helga. 'And that is very unusual.'

She is here because a Jesuit priest told her, when she was in despair, 'The most precious gift you can give to yourself is forgiveness of others.'

'He was right,' she said, pouring chai into the steel cups at the tea circle on my first day at Shantivanam. 'And it's only Jesus who talks about forgiveness. I've been through them all: Hinduism, Buddhism, New-Age-ism of all sorts. But only that man Jesus...'

Tears came, and I don't know why she went on. She had been in India for years, and into everything. Immediately before coming to Shantivanam, she was beaten within an inch of her life outside the main gates of her previous ashram ('a real Shiva place'). Members of the ashram stood by and watched. 'They didn't have to pay to go to the movies that night.' She insists that the teeth that were knocked out were miraculously implanted, but observed, to show that she wasn't mad, that 'it would have been nice if this miraculous power had defused his anger or deflected his blows'. With the first steps at forgiveness came the first signs of healing. 'I am beginning to heal. I practise forgiveness. When I am strong I feel that I can do it myself. But when I'm not – and that's most of the time – I cry out for help. And, quietly, it comes.

I'd been to Shantivanam before, but now — now that I know the desperation and urgency of my need — I know for the first time that I am really at home.'

Everywhere, in the really desperate of India, there is this instinctive crying out for grace to a God who is not themselves. 'I'm sick of wisdom,' says Helga. 'I know that wherever the answers are, they are not in me, and not in any books.'

Brother Martin would have disliked her dismissal of wisdom, but approved her dismissal of books. He was fond of reminding us that the Indian tradition is a 'wisdom' tradition — in which humans grope towards God; and he plainly thought that it had produced better results than the Hebrew tradition, in which God, on his own initiative, grabs at man with the jealous hands of a concerned mother.

In the musty library at Shantivanam, amongst the books hoarded by Bede and corroded by the rain, I had another look at the classical 'wisdom' books of the Bible. This time I found their hopeless internal inconsistency and their cynicism about their own contents exhilarating: these were wisdom books designed specifically to say that wisdom books got you nowhere. 'Meaningless! Meaningless!' said the philosopher of Ecclesiastes, 'Utterly meaningless! Everything is meaningless.... I applied myself to the understanding of wisdom, and also madness and folly, but I learned that this, too, is a chasing after the wind.' Systems fail; creeds disappoint; forces let you down. Only Personality endures, and hence relationships. And if the Christians are right,

Personality was there at the beginning and will be there at the end.

~

'I'm frightened of leaving here,' said Helga. 'I'm being hunted.'

Her mind was roughly opened, like a bad tin-opener hacks open a can, in a deep meditation session in Nepal. 'It took me to the depths of my subconscious,' she said, one dark night, choosing the shadow so that I could not see her panic as she told me the story. 'My teacher could not follow me there. I had no guide. To begin with it was wonderful. I had for four months what people on LSD have for two hours.' Dazzling lights flashed on and off in her head; there was unsullied bliss. The world was full of rainbows and kaleidoscopic colours. She also had extraordinarily heightened perception. 'I didn't hear noises in my ears, I felt them deep inside my body. My body resonated with everything outside me. I could see at night with UV vision, like an owl. I could make people do whatever I wanted. If I wanted someone to move, I'd just move my arm in the direction I wanted, and they would move. I knew – I could see – all the meridians and pressure points in people, and how those lines and points related, and why. I had the wisdom of ages. And then it started to get frightening.'

It was a hot night, and dark, with little moon. We were sitting on a wall. I felt her shiver. 'I went to the toilet. A bug fell into the toilet and died. I raised my eyebrow, and the dead bug moved its eye on the same side. I did this again and again, with my eyebrow and other parts of my body, and each time the corresponding part of the bug moved too. It then flew away. I didn't want power like this: I didn't know where it came from, what it would do to me, or how to get rid of it.'

For a while, though, there was just a light sprinkling of fear on the surface of the bliss. Real darkness came suddenly when a Danish woman at the ashram was murdered.

'They were looking for her body. I knew exactly where it was, but was frightened of saying, in case they thought I was the murderer. I know, too, that they have imprisoned the wrong person for the murder. This woman's spirit, or whatever it is, knowing that I am finely attuned to the things of the spirit, won't let me alone. She has attached herself to me like a vampire, sucking out my peace and my sleep, urging me all the time to expose the real killer. I keep telling her to go away, that I can't help, and her hold on me is weakening. She finds it hard to get inside the walls of prayer at Shantivanam.'

The darkness deepened.

'There was death wherever I looked. Wherever I was, it smelt of putrefaction. When a cat killed a mouse outside the house it left rivers of blood that seeped under my door. I walked out into the garden, and a bird fell dead from the branches, right into my path.'

Her relationships died too.

'My boyfriend told me that he wanted to sleep with other women, and he brought them back to sleep in our bed. I was so low and so fearful of being alone that I tolerated it at first, but finally I burned the mattress on which we'd slept together and on which he'd slept with all the other women. He beat me badly. The police did nothing. Later, two other men beat me up too.'

Her isolation was complete. She was at the ashram for two years, but made no friends. No one talked to her. If people from the ashram saw her walking in the town, they crossed the road to avoid her.

'I was desolate. I wanted to kill myself, but didn't know how to do it painlessly. I was terrified of more pain. I had nowhere to turn. Meditation plunged me still deeper into the dark. When I emerged from a meditation session it was like being underwater. All sounds were far off. When I lay down to sleep in a light and noisy room, there was a profound dark, as if I were dead. I felt that I was a particular Jewish girl being persecuted by the Nazis. I don't know if this was me in a past life – if there is such a thing – but I felt that I was somehow mopping up her pain.'

But she could not run. There was something that wouldn't let her.

'In all the two years, despite all the rejection, the fear and the violence, I couldn't spend a night outside the ashram. If I went away to Pondicherry, I'd be despairingly dragged back, as if by a huge, malignant magnet.'

Eventually, though, she did escape. She climbed on a bus to a town a long way away. As the bus bumped away, the darkness began to lift, and by the time she got off, the light was dazzling.

'It was my birthday, and everybody there, though they'd never seen me before, seemed to know it. Strangers hugged me and gave me gifts.'

From there she came to Shantivanam.

'I'm safer here, but even here the fear finds me. Wherever I go, people, like dogs, smell my fear. And outside Shantivanam people, like dogs, bite the fearful.'

She pointed at the sky. It was a glorious cloudless night.

'Look at those stars. People look up and say, "How beautiful!" But I feel scared. What will the stars do to me? They are not too far away to smell the fear, and stars have teeth.'

Outside my room there was a three-headed plaster statue depicting, as you chose, Saccidananda, the Holy Trinity, or innominate multi-valent power. An incense-stick was planted in the ground before it. Smoke coiled up into the eyes of the statue, sometimes blocking the light from the hurricane lamp, and all six eyes blinked.

When I left Shantivanam everyone smiled, and waved, and nobody asked me where I was going, because it was my business and not theirs.

～

*Chapter 10*

# THE MEETING OF THE SEAS

'For when there is duality, as it were, then one sees another, one smells another, one tastes another, one speaks to another, one hears another, one thinks of another, one touches another, one knows another. But when to the knower of Brahman everything has become the Self, then what should he see and through what? What should he smell and through what? What should he taste and through what? What should he speak and through what? What should he hear and through what? What should he think and through what? What should he touch and through what? What should he know and through what? Through what should one know That owing to which all this is known? This Self is That which has been described as 'Not this, not this.'

— Brihadaranyaka Upanishad IV, 5:15,
Trans. Swami Nikhilananda

∽

I went, in fact, to India's southern tip – to Kanyakumari, where the three seas meet. The pilgrims here cluster on the balconies at dawn. They greet the sun with a round of applause. Bells ring and boat horns sound. I rolled over resentfully and picked up a P.G. Wodehouse novel. It was the right book for the Indian Cape. Kanyakumari's a happy, tacky, carnival place. Most people are on a holiday lightly disguised as a pilgrimage. The men are in crisply ironed check shorts; the women in their brightest saris and their most dazzling nose studs. They all wallow and splash merrily in the ghats, just as they would in any provincial swimming pool. It's sometimes fun, as a Hindu, being redeemed.

Just off the mainland, accessible by boat after a nightmarish queue in a simmering tunnel of unaccountably cheerful people, are two over-photographed monuments. At the Vivekananda memorial, a podgy devotee of Sri Aurobindo, the charismatic guru of Pondicherry, stood in the queue for the boat back. He took reverently out of a brown paper bag a yoga manual, full of diagrams of lithe young men in shorts executing manoeuvres that never, in a thousand incarnations, would be remotely possible for my man. The coloured medical diagrams had English captions. Everything else was in Tamil. He saw me looking over his shoulder, and wobbled his head in greeting. It took the usual form.

'Where you from?'

'Israel,' I said. I'd found that that usually stopped touts, because they think that Israelis have no money to throw away, or are too smart to be fooled.

'That is good. And, please, what is your good name? I am Ashok.'

I told him the name of a lawyer friend from Tel Aviv, feeling bad, because Ashok seemed simply to be friendly.

'I see you looking at my book. Perhaps you are searching?'

'Aren't we all?'

'Very true. Very true. What do you look for? Perhaps I can take you there?'

I came to like this very much indeed about India – that you could go in a single sentence from asking a name to asking one's life's purpose. In London it would have taken years and a dozen drunken dinner parties. 'I'm still looking for the right questions,' I said, non-committally.

'Very good, very good. I've been looking for many years and now,' he tapped the book, 'I have found.'

'Found what?'

'I know who I am.'

'And who is that?'

The conversation was interrupted by the arrival of the boat and the wild stampede past the absurd signs saying, 'Passengers should embark and disembark in an ordered fashion, one by one.' A tiny man with a wasted leg, knocked flat and trampled, looked up and laughed toothlessly. India's a theatre of cruel slapstick. Wherever you look, emaciated men in loincloths are falling off bicycles, vanishing down holes in the road, being pulled screaming behind auto-rickshaws, absent-mindedly putting their hands into flailing machinery, being savaged by dogs or stepping barefoot in the piles of human dung that are everywhere.

'We will continue, please, on the mainland,' Ashok had screamed, seeing a convert in his sights, as the tide of bodies had separated us on the boat. And so we did, in a darkened café, muggy with incense and pulsating with ritual drums on a sticking tape.

I'd come across Ashok's master, Sri Aurobindo, before. Of his genius there is no doubt. He psychologised the Upanishads, and indeed many other strands of Indian thought, recasting them in Jungian language. Many of his insights were dazzling. Ashok, who worked as a software engineer in Bangalore, had spent every vacation in the past decade, apart from this one, at Aurobindo's ashram in Pondicherry. As Ashok rhapsodised about Aurobindo and the ashram, I remembered how I'd been there myself.

As I got off the bus at the Pondicherry bus station, my rucksack had burst open, scattering books everywhere. I crawled around, picking them up, and saw a pair of very comely ankles. They turned out to be attached to a pair of very comely legs in saffron pyjama trousers, and at the top of an equally comely torso was a perfectly acceptable head. These all belonged to Katrina, a German teacher who was staying in one of the ashram guest houses. 'This is yours, I think?' she said, and handed me an old notebook, half filled with pressed flowers from the Himalayas. She saw them, and they seemed to convince her that I was a sensitive, trustworthy soul, for she arranged for me to stay in another of the guest houses, and suggested, although I'd told her very quickly and deliberately about my unshakeable devotion to my wife and children, that I should go with her to a meditation session at the ashram. I went, and while we were drinking tea afterwards, she gave me the same lecture that Ashok was giving me. It was a lot more convincing coming from those lips, though.

Aurobindo, she said, was a great prophet, the perfect pilot through the dangerous waters of the psyche. With him at her helm, she felt confident and ambitious. There was nowhere in the collective unconscious that he had not been and had not mapped. There was nothing he had not felt and understood. His control over himself and his environment was supreme. When he died, on 5 December 1950, it was because he had chosen to die then. She quoted the Mother (Aurobindo's co-guru): 'Our Lord has sacrificed himself totally for us... He was not compelled to leave his body, he chose to do so for reasons so sublime that they are beyond the reach of human mentality.'

It was this that broke Katrina's potent spell. For I noted quietly to myself, with an unworthy schoolboy snigger, that Aurobindo had not had such sublime control when, a few years earlier, he tripped on a tiger-skin rug, landing on its snarling head and shattering his leg. He attributed this to the action of dark, elemental forces, desperate to stop his yogic mission.

That mission, like Bede's, was a consequence of childhood repression in and by middle-class England. Sent there as a boy by his stoutly Anglophilic parents, he was systematically denied all contact with Indian thought and culture. The idea was to turn him into a pillar of Empire – a well-scrubbed Indian Civil Servant – very civil, very servile and not at all Indian. But when he came back to India, India came back to him with a mystic force that engulfed in a moment everything that Cambridge had taught him. He steeped himself in the Vedas and the Upanishads, and then went hell for leather for 'Enlightenment'. Like languages, mathematics and examination marks, it came to him very quickly. His yoga teacher had told him simply to empty his mind, and that is what he did. When he saw thoughts coming, he tossed them out. 'In three days,' he wrote, 'I was free... In seven days I got the Nirvana experience which remained with me for a long time. I could not have got out of it even if I'd wanted to. Even afterwards this experience remained in the background in the midst of all activities.' Despite his colossal reading in mysticism and Hindu philosophy, nothing prepared him for its intensity. It '...made me see with a stupendous intensity the world as a cinematographic play of vacant forms in the impersonal universality of the Absolute Brahman.'

Katrina and Ashok were keen to emphasise Aurobindo's brilliance, his immense powers of concentration, his astonishing physical stamina. What they were less ready to tell me was that he was really not very nice. His most polished literary style was invective, of which he was a master. In his (entirely understandable) Indian nationalism, he was loudly dismissive of Gandhi, and he coordinated violent opposition to British rule. Indeed he was ideologically far closer to Nietzsche than to Gandhi, believing that in India a spiritual master race would arise. His adoring disciples at Pondicherry were guinea pigs in his plan for that race. A disciple wrote to him, 'Looking around and at one's self, one heaves a sigh and says: what disciples we are, of what a Master! I wish you had chosen or called some better stuff.' The response was chilling: 'As to the disciples, I agree! Yes, but would the better stuff, supposing it to exist, be typical of humanity? To deal with a few exceptional types would hardly solve the problem. And would they consent to follow my path – that is another question. And if they were put to the test, would not the common humanity suddenly reveal itself – that is still another question.'

You wouldn't trust him to look after your cat.

Aurobindo was fascinated by power, and didn't seem to mind too much where it came from. He was an occultist, obsessed with appropriating spiritual power. Some of his books were apparently dictated to him in the form of 'automatic writing' at séances.

He was not lacking in self-confidence. 'Sri Krishna has shown me the true meaning of the Vedas,' he wrote. 'He has also shown me the meaning of all in the Upanishads that is not understood either by Indians or Europeans. I have therefore to re-explain the whole Vedanta and Veda in such a way that it will be seen how all religion arises out of it and is one everywhere. In this way it will be proved that India is the centre of the religious life of the world and its destined saviour through the Sanatana Dharma.'

There's something creepily messianic about all this. There's no doubt that he saw himself as some sort of anointed one. He was encouraged in this belief by 'the Mother', the French mystic, who had had an occult, out-of-body meeting with a teacher whom she called 'Krishna'. When she travelled to Pondicherrry and met Aurobindo she immediately recognised him as 'Krishna': '...I was aware that it was with him... that the divine work was to be done.'

'With the Mother's arrival,' wrote a disciple, in one of the breathlessly adoring hagiographies to be bought in the ashram bookshop, 'there was a mighty mingling of two vast streams of *sadhana* which Sri Aurobindo and the Mother were pursuing individually. These now joined forever to mark the beginning of a new era of spiritual creation: "An hour began, the matrix of new Time."'

Each fuelled the extraordinary self-belief of the other, and yet the Mother always seems to have been a sort of John the Baptist figure – preparing the way for the saving grace of Aurobindo. Every religious movement needs *history*, needs events, and Sri Aurobindo's climatic moment was 24 November 1926 – the day that became known as the Day of Siddhi. 'This,' said Katrina ominously, 'was the time when all excuses for not believing in Aurobindo vanished.' 'This,' said Ashok, with rolling eyes, 'was the day when all the power we could ever need landed in Pondicherry.'

Something was expected to happen. That seems generally important in Indian epiphanies. The disciples were on tenterhooks. 'The presence of the Higher Power began to be unbearable,' wrote one. 'Many saw an oceanic flood of light rushing down from above. Everyone present felt a kind of pressure above his head. The whole atmosphere felt surcharged with some electrical energy… it was certain that a Higher Consciousness had descended on earth…'

It had descended, of course, into Aurobindo himself. Krishna himself had entered Aurobindo. Aurobindo wrote, '24 November 1926 is the day when Sri Krishna descended into the body. His descent means the descent of the Overmind God which will prepare the descent of the Supermind.'

'So you see,' said Katrina, pressing doggedly on, 'this is the place to be. This is where it all happened, and where it's all going to happen.'

'What's going to happen?'

'The creation of the new world; a new consciousness; reconciliation between ourselves and the divine, which will mean reconciliation between ourselves and ourselves, and between ourselves and nature. Ego will end here; selfishness will end here.'

'So how's it going?'

'Well. Very well. Of course there's much work to do, but we've taken great strides towards the new creation.'

Ashok agreed. 'We are well on our way to rebuilding the world.'

Aurobindists sought to model the new order in Auroville, just north of Pondicherry – an amorphous cluster of settlements and ethical businesses with, at its centre, a huge golden golf ball in which the Aurovillians meditate the Kingdom of Heaven into existence in themselves. Apparently happy, apparently balanced and very thin twenty-something basket-weaving couples buzz laughing round Auroville on Vespas, swerving round the apparently desolate, lost-looking fifty-something females who do the cooking. It's a place of no compromise with modernity (bar the Vespas and the glitzy Visitor Centre), capitalism (bar the immensely shrewd export and mark-up policy for its splendid hand-made goods), worldly jealousies (if you forget the acrimonious and long-standing feud with the Sri Aurobindo ashram over Aurovillian jurisdiction, which reached the secular courts of India) or European plumbing. Bob Dylan presides at every meal, the Beatles are in heaven and all is well with the world.

Aurobindo died in 1950. But apparently he didn't just die. Aurobindo never did anything quite the way that anyone else did. When he stumbled over that rug, he was pushed by malicious demons. And his death was somehow a sacrifice: '...the total significance of this supreme sacrifice,' wrote the bookshop biographer, 'will remain ungrasped by our limited intelligence. His body was suffused with a crimson-gold light. Power and peace and bliss filled the room... Untarnished, undimmed, for five days the body lay in state...'

Katrina and I sat in the main courtyard of the ashram, looking at the tombs of Aurobindo and the Mother, which lie side by side, covered in flowers and uncritical adulation. Many members of the ashram were meditating around the tomb.

'Why are they meditating here?' I whispered.

Katrina looked at me, obviously thinking I was completely stupid. 'Because they are buried here,' she said, shaking that delightful head.

The Mother penned a prayer which is inscribed on Aurobindo's tomb: 'To thee, who has been the material envelope of our Master,' she wrote. 'To thee our infinite gratitude.'

Ashok choked loudly on his onion *bhaji*, which brought me back to Kanyakumari. I thumped him brutally on the back and knocked all his pens from his breast pocket. Adeptly he turned it into a parable.

'These pens represent the useless accumulated thoughts of my past. You came along like Aurobindo and, out of compassion, gave me a blow which emptied me of all the rubbish.'

He picked up all his pens and replaced them carefully.

On the bus going out of Kanyakumari there was a dazzlingly lovely girl with flowers in her hair, immaculately made up, earnestly highlighting a handwritten handout called 'Human effluent: the basics.' It's impossible not to like this country very much indeed.

So why are all the long-term Western travellers here worn, harassed and *running* in a way that's unusual amongst travellers in Asia? There's more transcendental calm in Disneyland than in the backpackers' doss-houses backing onto the big pilgrimage sites of India. Whatever they're looking for, they haven't found it, or if they have, it's not doing them much good, and they'd be better off asking in a New Jersey mall. Most of the women are unhappily unmarried and of a certain age. They wear their Indian cotton trousers as badges of defiance, but the desperation shows; desperation to know that there are bigger and more glorious boats than the ones they've missed; jewelled boats going to exotic destinations of which the tragic housewives of the suburbs could never dream. They need to know that air-con, children and a company pension scheme are demonic lies. Except that there are no such things as demons, of course; just shadows flickering in the catacombs of your psyche, which vanish when the guru hits the switch and lets his light in. Or perhaps the light has gone on, and they've seen, as I saw in myself once, a queasily vertiginous emptiness.

I sat on the laughably named Super-Express Deluxe bus, watching fat men woo and win beautiful women on the sub-titled video. 'If she becomes an ice cream,' counselled one singer, in quarter tones, 'become a spoon.' 'A satellite knows about the earth's fertility,' a moustachioed Romeo assured his beloved, as he leapt unwisely between some Mogul battlements, 'my palm knows your features.' It seemed to work as a chat-up line, for she immediately urged him, 'Come to dash your nose with mine.'

Randy, a fifty-five-year-old reformed real estate agent from Nashville, clambered onto the bus and slung himself down beside me. I pretended to be asleep, but the video was too fascinating, and he found me out. A few miles down the road he tried to rummage through my soul, and when I said no, took his out and started talking me through it.

He'd been in India a good deal. He knew a lot of the language of Hinduism, and sprayed it incontinently around. He hated silence, and wore his mystical experiences like a cheerleader's hat.

'Have you tried *peyote*? You must. Everyone should.'

I sighed, hoping but not believing for a moment that a display of unconcern might spare me from a predictably excruciating hour. 'Not really my sort of thing.'

'I thought that myself. I did. But am I glad that I thought again? I am indeed. I'll never be the same again. No I won't.'

I suspected that was true. I looked longingly at the video, where a couple were skipping round a tree singing, 'You are my first rain. You are the first tide in my heart. I was a dry leaf until you touched me. When you touched, I grew wings.'

'It did different things to me every time,' Randy was saying. 'The first time, I was beneath the earth. The earth was a sort of womb, and I was waiting to be born from it. Then I shape-shifted into an anaconda, writhed my way through the earth, through a mulch of damp leaves and into the air, where I flickered my tongue and tasted the tang of white light.'

The video relationship had hit rocky times: 'We asked for flowers,' the weeping girl was moaning, 'who threw these pebbles? I want to pull down the cloud, spread it in a basket, and sleep in the sky.' I knew how she felt.

Randy pressed on. 'The light was split by my forked tongue into the two genders. A rainbow man and a rainbow woman copulated. My tongue was there at the beginning. I hissed mankind into existence.'

We passed a bus called *The Flaying Palace*.

'Then, the second time, I was an eagle. I could feel the lift, and I saw the basketball hall where the group had been given the peyote falling away as I rose. I could see mice beneath the boards, and I wanted to kill.'

Things were still turbulent on the video. Romeo was at the airport, bellowing at Juliet's jumbo jet, which had just taken off: 'We loved the rain. Did we ask for a storm?'

The bus stopped at the Asia Big Chicken Centre, a roadside shack that sold tea and bananas, but not chicken.

'And then, my friend, I saw Durga. She was riding on a tiger. She had a whip in her hand, and she beat the woods through which she rode. At the touch of the lash, the layers of the trees and grasses stripped off, just like in a biology textbook, exposing the xylem and the phloem, and massively magnifying all the tissues. First I saw each cell, and then the workings of each cell; the biochemical production line of the mitochondria; the uncoiling of the DNA strands; even mutation at a molecular level as sun knocked out a molecule here and a molecule there.'

There had been some sort of reconciliation at another airport. 'You've encased my soul in your dimple,' the fat chap was telling the girl, who was taking it all in her stride. 'Who are you? Who am I? Are you the mirage?' This at least was a good point.

'Amazing things began to happen then,' came the drawl from my right. 'Amazing things. I just can't bring myself to talk about them.'

I think he was lying. I don't think there's anything he wouldn't have spoken about. 'I'll tell you this, though,' he went on, 'I saw the archetypes of all the great religions.'

'Archetypes?'

'Yep,' he said, as if it were all self-explanatory.

If he'd been telling the truth, he'd have expounded and expanded. I waited, but he looked hurt that I'd interrupted. It was as if I'd stepped blasphemously onto holy ground with unwashed feet.

'It's made me a searcher.'

'A searcher? I'd have thought that all that amounted to finding.'

He swelled with the peculiar, and peculiarly emetic, pride that that comes when someone is about to be humble and self-deprecating. 'I suppose you're right. But you can always press on harder and further, and search for ways to help others along the road you've travelled yourself.'

The video couple were united, and were probably managing a cellphone franchise in Mysore by now. They had given way to a sterner, more philosophical pair, who were assuring one another, amid lots of almost-but-not-quite-pelvic-thrusting, that 'our caste differences are because of our ancestors'. Once they'd got that out of the way, they felt able to move on quite quickly to the magnificently mixed romantic metaphors of Tamil cinema: 'A flower comes with swaying arms. Your eyes started to blaze. Why this heat in the vicinity of your eyes?' And then to the very legalistic bottom line: 'If you give consent we can exchange our bodies.'

'Sad, isn't it,' said Randy, motioning at the video. 'They've exchanged all the culture of the last five thousand years for this.'

We pulled into the bus station. I saw him later in town. He was buying a copy of *Playboy* magazine. He saw that I'd noticed, coloured, and blustered: 'Nearest thing to those temple carvings, eh? Published in India by Lord Shiva himself.' He laughed nervously and scuttled off to his hotel.

~

*Chapter 11*

# LUNCH WITH ADVAITA

'*My idea of God is not a divine idea. It has to be shattered time after time. He shatters it himself. He is the great iconoclast. Could we not almost say that this shattering is one of the marks of his presence? ...All reality is iconoclastic. The earthly beloved, even in this life, incessantly triumphs over your mere idea of her.*'

– C.S. Lewis
*A Grief Observed*

∼

India *seethes*. You see that almost immediately. Often you see nothing else, and it can revolt. What happens when you stay here for a while is that you realise that the seething is actually a dance to a deep, low rhythm. At first you can't hear the rhythm; you deduce it by seeing the synchronicity of the seethes. But then you feel it shuddering up from the hot earth, and if you can be still enough and relaxed enough, you begin to shudder with it. It would probably take several lifetimes to oscillate properly with this or any place (and indeed the Hindu reincarnationists say that it does), but the process can be speeded up by fishing, hatha yoga, walking barefoot and drinking palm beer. Also, according to everyone, by going to see Kathakali, the ritualised dance of Kerala.

This was supposed to be life-changing. Bede Griffiths had gone into epistolic ecstasies over it: 'It'll teach you, like nothing else on earth, the real nature of myth,' he had written. All those years ago, Badri had said: 'It'll blow the dust from all those childhood legends, and the dust will never settle again.' So I obediently bought a ticket and was ushered into a little, hot theatre three quarters of an hour before the performance was due to start. 'You need to see the make-up,' Badri had urged me. 'The transformation of ordinary, workaday individuals into demons and goddesses is all part of the myth-making. The myth *lives* because of the reality of the transformation.'

I wasn't sure that I understood this, but certainly there was nothing workaday about the crew performing that night. One of them had two thumbs on his left hand. The main thumb was massively enlarged, and out of it sprouted a smaller, feminine, perfectly formed and well-manicured second thumb, which seemed to be useful when he was gluing cardboard jowls to a demon's face. I was transfixed. It boded well for the rest of the show.

One of the first dances was supposed to represent the creation dance of Lord Shiva. If I were a Hindu, I'd have found it riot-engenderingly blasphemous. A genial, podgy chap with a neat side parting, bells on his ankles, an expression like a llama, very approximately shaved armpits and lots of lipstick lumbered around roughly in time to some drumming. Every so often, a bloke in a check shirt and tight nylon trousers would wander into the wings, obviously unaware he could be seen by everyone, and make obscene gestures to one of the handmaidens of Vishnu poised to come on next. This next dance, a booming commentary told us, was 'naughtily erotic'. We braced ourselves for the tidal wave of lust that was to burst over us. We needn't have bothered. Three sturdy bus-conductress types stomped up and down, pretended to sniff roses, and then filed moodily out. One of them had evidently aroused the man in the nylon trousers, but his were strange, inscrutably oriental tastes.

And so it went on. We were treated to a display of Kalaripayattu, the ancient martial art of Kerala, which requires, the commentator assured us, 'a devoted lifestyle, to ensure that body and soul are in perfect harmony'. There was some drumming, no one came on, and the drummers gave up. Then there was some sort of signal from the wings, the drummers started again, and three sweating bouncer-types in black shirts leapt on stage and started belabouring each other with sticks. There were moans as they hit each others' hands, and then they bowed off, plainly relieved it was over, to be replaced by a wiry little man in platform shoes who whirled some poles round his head for a while. Inevitably the poles clashed, and one of them span out into the audience, landing with a sickening crash.

'I think he's broken my chutney, George,' wailed a woman from Alabama. And he had. An anxious manager rushed forward, assured George that the chutney would be replaced with the compliments of the management, and the show went on. And on.

There was lots of kit involved, and so it's not surprising that some of it went wrong. Masks fell off, bells scuttered across the floor, greasepaint was smeared and cardboard jowls came adrift, despite having had the benefit of an extra thumb. A sort of Eastern Widow Twanky demonstrated the facial grimaces which, together with an elaborate hand semaphore, make up the grammar of Kathakali. Then the demons, the bus conductresses, the good widow and the llama did a not tremendously grand finale, and it was all over.

The whole thing was marvellous. I wouldn't have changed a stomp or a note of it. On the way out I looked in the visitors' book. Many of the people in that audience had made comments as they left. They must have been reading Bede Griffiths, and had their fingers firmly on the mystic pulse of India. 'Moving and evocative,' someone had written. 'A thrilling trip into the heart of Hindu mythology.' Even George had written, 'Never has chutney been spilt in so good a cause. Thank you from the bottom of our hearts for opening our eyes.' He didn't say to what, of course, but I assume it wasn't what I'd seen.

I was almost at the end of my time in India, and had no real idea what I'd seen here. I was sometimes alarmed and sometimes relieved by the discrepancy between my experience and the ones I read about.

I went out into the night, walked down to the waterfront, bought a fish from one of the Chinese-net fishermen, and took it along to a restaurant to be cooked. I sat at a corner table, intermittently reading and looking out onto the sea. A wind came at us from Arabia, and I knew where I had to go the next day. But first, that night, I needed to see Raj.

Raj is the kind of man who knows everything. If you want to know the bulk price of cinnamon, or where to find the cheapest shark, or the safest gynaecologist, he's your man. But he's no mere barrow boy. Before he was sent down from Oxford for running an unlicensed tyre importation business from his college rooms, he picked up a good deal of philosophy, along with a taste for vintage Burgundy and Crusader castles. The shelves of his crumbling Portuguese house in Mattancherry are lined with Eckhart, Rilke, Hesse and Sanskrit grammar. He wears Italian shirts and smells of cardamom. A few years ago, to the immense surprise of his business partners, his numerous Oxford girlfriends and himself, he turned Christian.

I'd met him at Beirut airport, where he was the only person wearing tartan trousers, and when it turned out that he wanted to write about the Celtic saints who had lived on prayer, rainwater and gannet meat on the Outer Hebrides, I knew I'd found a friend. The trousers were misleading. He was one of the most serious people I knew, and he seriously knew how to have fun. He had studied fun, as he studied everything. His letters were luminous with his love of seabirds, orchids, Arabic calligraphy, embalming techniques, sailing boats, the biology of plankton and the Gnostic gospels.

When I saw him in Kochi he had just started Spanish evening classes, and had spent almost a month's income importing small mammal traps so that he could survey the mice, shrews and voles on his uncle's banana plantation.

After he had opened three bottles of something rare from the Cote de Nuits and declared one of them good enough, he waved me away from the bookcase to a chair where he could watch me over the top of his glass. And that's what he did. He listened in perfect silence as I talked incoherently and for hours, obviously troubled, about the Vedas, the Dhammapada, *atman*, the monks of Shantivanam, Emily's legs, the eternal fate of street sweepers, the birth and evolution of myth, the need for blood sacrifice, tsunamis, disabled children, stone footprints, the apotheosis of Aurobindo, peyote, coconut offerings, holy mountains, thought-journeys, swifts and psalms.

At the end of it all he said simply: 'Christianity is the business of having lunch with advaita.'

~

# EPILOGUE

'I'd not give way for an Emperor,
I'd hold my road for a King—
To the Triple Crown I would not bow down—
But this is a different thing.
I'll not fight with the Powers of the Air,
Sentry, pass him through!
Drawbridge let fall, 'Tis the Lord of us all.
The Dreamer whose dreams come true.'

– Rudyard Kipling
*The Fairies' Siege*

~

I took a car again out to Kodangallur. This time I was on my own. I paid off the driver and walked along a sandy road through the banana plantations to the edge of India. Clouds were piling up over the sea. One small boat was playing in the hot wind. I threw my bag down at the foot of a tree, and threw myself after it. And there I stayed, drinking water and looking out over the sea, for a night and a day. The wind dropped with the light, and just touched my face gently. I tried to watch the sea all night – it seemed important to watch – but the roll and crash lulled me, and I must have slept.

The wind still came from the north west. It rose in the Empty Quarter of Arabia, as the heat smashed into the sand and made the air reel back into the sky, spiralling high and sucking into its vortex the scented air of Jerusalem. It was a wind like this that filled the sails of Thomas's boat. He brought Jerusalem with him in more ways than one. About nineteen years before he had looked into the blazing eyes of a man who, he believed, had been most emphatically dead and buried.

As so often, I didn't know what I was watching for.

~